FineScale MODELER

ARMOR CONVERSION AND DETAILING PROJECTS

from FineScale Modeler magazine

KALMBACH BOOKS

Publisher's Cataloging in Publication
(Prepared by Quality Books, Inc.)

      Armor conversion and detailing projects /
editor, Terry Spohn.
      p. cm.
      Including bibliographical references.
      ISBN 0-89024-268-2

      1. Models and modelmaking. 2. Armored vehicles, Military—Models. I. Spohn, Terry, ed.

TT154.A76 1995   745.5'928
                        QBI95-20285

Book Design: Kristi Ludwig

CONTENTS

MODELING THE FIRST SHERMAN TANK

An M4 conversion in 1/35 scale

Lee's early M4 Sherman shows off the sand-cast look of the turret and plain proving ground markings.

BY LEE THOMAS

The Sherman tank wasn't the biggest or the best, but it was relentless in both numbers and reliability. It carved its name in history, "Built like a Sherman tank!" The Sherman rivals the Russian T-34 as the most-produced tank in history; more than 49,000 were built. I wanted to build the first of the line, an M4. (The M4 wasn't the first version produced—the M4A1 and the M4A2 actually came off the production lines earlier—but the M4 was the first Sherman standardized as a production design.)

Research. Information on the M4 Sherman is a good-news bad-news situation. The good news is that many excellent books and articles exist dealing with the Sherman; the bad news is that none of these sources is definitive and you may need several publications to find details on a particular variant. Many examples of Shermans still exist and can be studied, but many of these are test vehicles, one-off modifications, or other deviations from production standards. I found only one photo of the particular version I was interested in, so I assume few actually were produced.

Monogram makes a nice early M4 in 1/32 scale, but I wanted my collection of Shermans to be in 1/35 scale, so extensive kitbashing

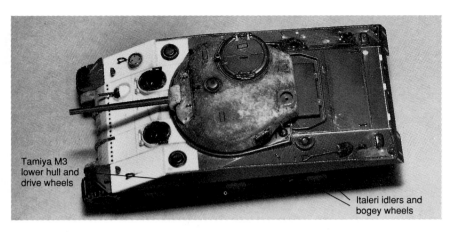

Tamiya M3 lower hull and drive wheels

Italeri idlers and bogey wheels

Fig. 1. PARTS BREAKDOWN

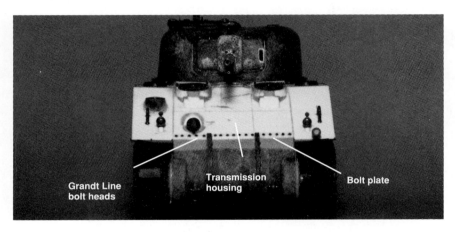

Grandt Line bolt heads

Transmission housing

Bolt plate

Fig. 2. The transmission was given a cast appearance and a new bolt plate detailed and faired into the front plate.

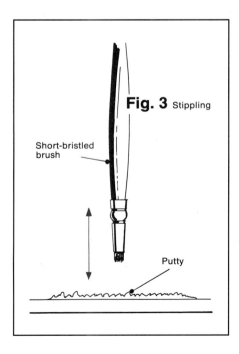

Fig. 3 Stippling

Short-bristled brush

Putty

Shermans this plate was simply machined metal with slight indentations for the bolts. Study photos and drawings to guide you here. I modified Grandt Line bolt and washer parts by trimming the washers to match the bolt shape, then drilled holes in a strip of .030" styrene to mount the bolts. This assembly was glued to the transmission and filled in, Fig. 2. The transmission was given a cast look by stippling auto glazing putty on the nonmachined areas.

Stippling is a simple way of applying cast texture to a surface. I use a large paintbrush (No. 7), and cut the bristles down to about 1/4" so they are stiff. Dab putty on the brush, then apply it with short strokes, perpendicular to the model surface, Fig. 3, to give a roughcast look. If the putty is too thick, use Testor's Liquid Cement as a thinner.

Use the rear bulkhead from the Italeri kit, trimmed to fit into the M3 hull. Cut off the rear idler axles and install Italeri axles, using styrene shims to help them fit. Fill the rear bulkhead mounting holes in the M3 hull and install Italeri idler wheels. Remove the outer guards on the rear towing lugs and install the C rings from the M3 kit. Filter cans are modified Fujimi parts with Italeri lock lugs installed, and the exhaust pipes are Italeri parts. Install a screen in the open area of the upper hull above the rear bulkhead.

Upper hull. This area requires the most work. Starting with the Tamiya M4A3 hull, remove the two forward engine deck plates and replace them with Italeri engine covers, Fig. 4. The Tamiya hull's rear plate must be shortened to allow the Italeri parts to fit. Early Shermans didn't have the

was required. Parts from four different kits were used: a Tamiya M4A3 (No. 35122), Tamiya M3 Lee or Grant (Nos. 35039 and 35041), Fujimi M4A1, and an Italeri M4A1 (No. 225), Fig. 1. This may seem extravagant, but the results were worth it, and the kits yielded spare parts which I used on other Sherman projects.

Lower hull. I began with the lower hull of the Tamiya M3 Lee or Grant. The front drive wheels are used without modification. Italeri M4A1 bogey wheels are used with their centers drilled to 7/64" to fit on the M3's bogey suspension. The transmission housing is assembled and a new bolt plate is fabricated. On early

extra filler cap found on Italeri's deck, so remove the cap and the Tamiya grab handles. Mounting holes, rear storage rack slots, and light-guard holes on the rear hull should be filled. Cut off the vents for the rear grouser storage areas from the Italeri hull; Tamiya left these vents off its M4, so mount the Italeri parts on the hull using photos as reference, Fig. 4.

Front hull. Starting where the front plate meets the bottom of the side plate, mark a line 35 degrees up along the side, Fig. 5. This is the cut line for an early Sherman hull. Carefully remove the front mud flaps and cut the existing front plate away, from just inside the hull side plates back to the weld line on the upper hull. Cut along the weld line to the turret splash ring and around the splash ring to remove the front plate. Clean up the splash ring to provide a good fit for the new upper hull plate.

Make the new upper plate from $2^{13}/16$" x $5/8$" .030" styrene, Fig. 6. Scribe the radius for the turret splash shield directly off the hull into the plate and cut it to fit. The front armor plate is

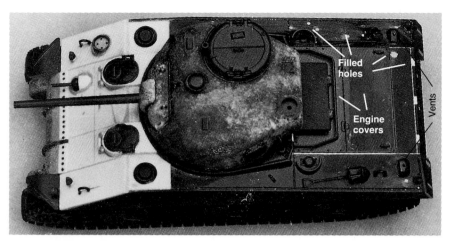

Fig. 4. The rear deck consists of Italeri engine covers and detail parts on a Tamiya hull.

Fig. 5. Remove the front of the Tamiya Sherman hull.

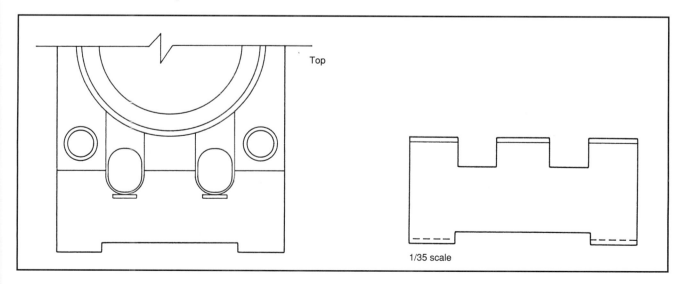

Fig. 6. FRONT AND TOP PLATE TEMPLATES

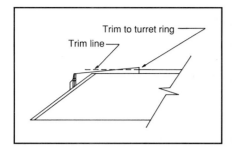

Fig. 7. HATCH COMBINGS

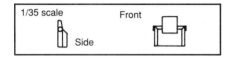

Fig. 9. VISION PORTS

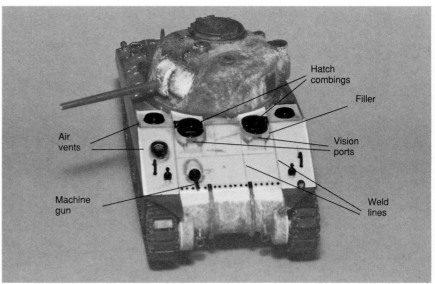

Fig. 8. Front hull details include the hatches and combings, machine gun, air vents, and weld lines.

3¹⁵⁄₁₆" x 1³⁄₈" cut from .040" styrene, Fig. 6. Glue this to the cut-down side plates and bevel the top and bottom to match the hull line. Cut a notch in the bottom of the front plate to fit around the transmission housing and glue sheet plastic behind this joint to add strength.

The trickiest part of the project is the front hatch combings, made from ½" x ¹⁵⁄₁₆" styrene. Fit Fujimi hatches to the combings, modifying the hinges with sprue cut to match the front contour. Be aware that the combings slope forward, but end in a vertical plane at the front, Fig. 7.

Cut slots ⁵⁄₈" in from each side and ½" wide in the front hull to accept the hatch combings, but don't cut the splash shield. Fit the combings, leaving them slightly higher than the splash shield. Once fitted, file them flat to match the shield and fill in the open front area, Fig. 8. I use Milliput epoxy putty for filling large areas; it doesn't shrink and can be worked with a wet finger while it cures.

Front hull details. The air vents on the upper front of the hull were

cut off a Tamiya Sherman turret. I drilled a large hole in the front glacis plate to accept Plastruct tubing which forms the machine gun mount. The vent is made the same way with a plastic skirt and Grandt Line bolt detailing added to the cap, Fig. 8. Delete the kit periscope guards, as these weren't found on early Shermans. The front vision ports are complex assemblies. Open up and flatten a ³⁄₈" area on the front of each combing, make the vision ports from plastic, Fig. 9, and slide them into place.

Form weld lines and plate seams on the front plate with auto glazing putty, Fig. 8. Welds are easily produced using putty; lay masking tape to outline the weld area and stipple putty over the open line. Pull the tape up while the putty is still wet; you can tap down overly large stippling with your finger, but don't flatten it.

Turret. Tamiya's M4A3 features the later high-bustle turret, so I used Fujimi's early turret. This turret isn't as well detailed as

Tamiya's, but it's usable with a few minor fixes. For starters, add a Tamiya pistol port and two-piece hatch, Fig. 10. Fujimi molded the latter .030 caliber machine gun shield to the mantlet; remove this shield and open up the slot to accept a machine gun barrel. Remember to position the machine gun at the same elevation as the main cannon.

I chose to replace the bolt flange detail around the gun mantlet and add slotted screws to the gun slot guard. Slot the ends of Grandt Line plastic rod using a razor saw and carefully insert the rods into drilled holes. Use the Tamiya 75 mm gun barrel and install lift lugs and other small details, Fig. 11. Stipple the entire turret for a sand-cast look.

Tracks. The tracks are the final part of the conversion. Italeri provides tracks with the correct plain rubber block pattern. Dipping the ends that go around the drive and idler wheels into boiling water lets you bend the tracks so they lie flat on the return wheels. Dip the end

Fig. 10. Lee added a Tamiya hatch, pistol port, and details to the Fujimi turret.

Fig. 11. Turret details include lift lugs, bolt detail on the mantlet, and the coaxial machine gun slot.

into the water while holding the track in the position you want but be careful not to overheat and melt the tracks. Practice on an old set if you've never tried this.

Painting and markings. I used Floquil olive drab as my base coat. Edges were sprayed with a lightened mixture of the same color.

After the paint has dried for a day or two, add the markings. Having a photo of an M3 at Aberdeen and a later M4A3, I split the difference to come up with test numbers for a vehicle in the M4 series. The only markings on most test vehicles from the early war period were blue equipment numbers and

white-stenciled four-digit numbers. These are sealed with a coat of my special flat mixture—50-50 Floquil flat and Humbrol matte clear, thinned with Dio-Sol. This mix is flat!

I added M. V. Products lenses for headlights and stained-glass window tints for the taillights. I painted Floquil gunmetal on the tracks and Tamiya acrylic flat black on the rubber track blocks.

Weathering. A test vehicle would not usually be loaded down with exterior equipment and should be clean and well maintained, so I kept my weathering light.

The first step is a wash of Gunze Sangyo flat black. Water down the paint so it acts as a stain and apply it to bring out details. Wipe off excess with a damp cloth and allow the wash to dry. I pour off the carrier and thinner from a bottle of Floquil Mud; this leaves a thick mud which is dry-brushed on the tracks and areas that would have mud splashed on them.

I lightly dry-brushed the entire tank with several shades of tan and green to age the paint. A light coat of Floquil dust was sprayed on the suspension and lower hull. Finally, apply light coats of gray, tan, yellow, and brown pastel chalks with a paintbrush. Now you have a vehicle that looks like it lives in the real world.

The base. I don't normally make bases for my aircraft models; their environment is the air, so I set them on glass shelves in my showcase. But a 30-ton vehicle looks silly on a piece of glass, so most of my armor is set on a base. This also helps me avoid touching the pastel surface, because the model can be moved by picking up the base.

I used a ready-made white pine base from a craft store. Sand it smooth, use a latex walnut stain, then spray three coats of polyurethane satin clear over the stain. Protect the edges by covering them with masking tape. I use a mix of Hydrocal plaster, water, and Polly S brown paint to produce tan mud. This mixture is troweled over the top of the base, then crushed stone is sprinkled and pushed into the plaster.

After the plaster dries, tint the dirt with a series of black, brown, and tan washes. Follow this with dry-brushed yellow and tan. Add some static grass by brushing watered-down white glue where you want the grass and sprinkling it on. Dry-brush the grass flat green and dust on tan, yellow, and green pastels. The entire base is dusted with pastels and the tank attached with contact cement.

That finishes an early M4 Sherman, but be careful; if Shermans get into your blood, you may never stop building them!

SOURCES
• **Grandt Line Products, Inc., 1040B Shary Court, Concord, CA 94518**
• **Milliput, Rosemont Hobby Shop, P.O. Box 139, Trexler Mall, Trexlertown, PA 18087**
• **M. V. Products, P.O. Box 6622, Orange, CA 92667**

REFERENCES
• **Culver, Bruce, *Sherman In Action,* Squadron/Signal Publications, Inc., Carrollton, Texas, 1977**
• **Ellis, Chris, and Peter Chamberlain, *Sherman Tank, 1941–1945 Production Models,* Almarks Publication, Edgwave, Middlesex, England, 1970**
• **Forty, George, *M4 Sherman,* Blandford Press, Poole, England, 1987**
• **Hunnicutt, R. P., Sherman, *A History of the American Medium Tank,* Taurus Enterprise, Belmonte, California, 1978**

MODELING A STALINGRAD T-34

An easy 1/35 scale conversion that tells a gripping tale

An unpainted STZ T-34/76 testifies to the bravery of Russian arms workers in the Battle of Stalingrad. Factory employees fought the German Sixth Army in their spare time.

BY JOE MORGAN

The battle of Stalingrad, fought from August 1942 to February 1943, was the beginning of the end for Adolf Hitler, who stubbornly underestimated Russia's fighting spirit. Russian resolve was exemplified by workers at Stalingrad's Dzerhezirsky Tractor Plant (STZ), who kept building tanks until their factory was overrun. According to legend, unpainted, barely equipped tanks were driven off the assembly line and straight into combat. That passage in the epic of Stalingrad inspired me to build this STZ T-34/76.

The kits. Visible differences between STZ T-34s and others produced at the same time include a simplified flat plate on the turret rear, flat plates at the lower front, and a pointed mantlet (instead of the blunt one made elsewhere).

Although Tamiya makes three T-34 variants, the STZ model is not among them. I built Tamiya's 1/35 scale 1943 Model T-34/76 (kit No. 35059). MB Models' conversion kit (No. 1063) provided the correct turret with hatch and ventilator, as well as distinctive hull plates.

Bottom up. The first order of business is to fill those pesky motorization holes that you find in the

bottom of Tamiya armor kits. The small slots in the middle are easy to cover: Plastruct styrene T shapes are just the right size. I smoothed the outside of the holes with Dr. Microtools epoxy putty.

Check your junk box for a part with a curve and bolt pattern that matches the surrounding molded detail (Fig. 1). I used scraps from a Tamiya Panzer IV. Close is good enough here—the area is hard to see after the tracks are fitted.

Lower rear hull plate. The MB Models conversion kit supplies a lower rear hull plate to replace Tamiya part A22 (Fig. 2). Slice off the semicircular locating flanges

Fig. 1. Fill slots with scrap styrene and epoxy putty; a spare part provides a missing link. Cut off the locating flange inside the lower hull.

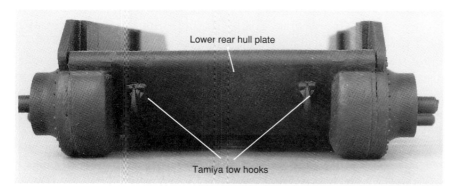

Fig. 2. MB Models' lower rear hull plate replaces Tamiya part A22.

Fig. 3. MB Models' rear upper hull plate features an early-style access hatch.

inside the lower hull and fill the locating slots at the top of the drive molding (Fig. 1). Cut off the molded tow hook brackets from the MB Models part, remove the locating pins from the kit tow hooks (A13), and super glue the hooks on the new hull plate (Fig. 2).

To be sure you have the lower hull plate perfectly placed, test fit it with the Tamiya kit's rear engine deck cover (A11) and the MB Models rear upper hull plate (Fig. 3). Mount Plastruct angle across the width of the inside lower hull, flush to the lower edge. This simplifies positioning the parts.

Upper hull and turret. The first order of business on the upper hull was filling the locating holes for stowed equipment.

Remember, this tank was rushed off the assembly line, so it would be missing most of the usual accessories. External fuel tanks would have been superfluous with the action so close at hand, so I filled the locating holes for those,

Brass mount

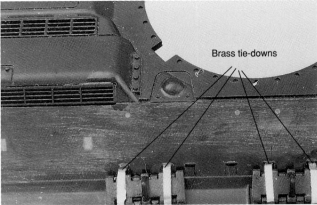

Brass tie-downs

Fig. 4. Joe made details like this headlight mount with scraps of photoetched brass.

Fig. 5. More details, more photoetched brass: Tie-downs hold spare track.

too. I backed the openings with scrap styrene and smoothed them with putty. I also filled locating holes for the grab handles (don't forget the four holes up front!) and the rear toolbox.

Headlights on STZ T-34s were mounted on the glacis plate rather than the hull side. I carefully shaved the molded electrical cable from the hull side, filled the mounting hole, and made a new

headlight mount from a leftover piece of photoetched brass (Fig. 4). I used the same material for spare-track tie-downs (Fig. 5). I also backdated the hull machine-gun mantlet: I replaced the ball with a recessed fitting, filling the slot and installing a Bren machine gun from my spares box (Fig. 6).

After fitting the machine gun I followed the kit instructions with only one more exception. I

cut the hook off the rear edge of the upper hull so it would fit with the resin rear-hull plate. Since I was stowing only the barest minimum of equipment, I completed the hull in record time. Your spare-parts box is going to love this conversion!

MB Models' turret is a beautiful casting that needs only minor touch-ups. Fill blemishes with putty, clean up the hatch and the gun barrel, fit three lifting hooks, and you're done.

Paint. It's ironic that it took me so long to paint an unpainted tank! The desired effect is rust—not scaled, rough, aged rust, but the patina of smooth rust that appears overnight on new steel. This is not a multi-bottle treatment, and you don't have to texture the surface.

First, I airbrushed everything including the tracks with Pactra hull red (NA21). I went back over the tank with a small brush and flat black, picking on recessed details such as engine grilles, gun bores, vision ports, and exhaust pipes. Next I dry-brushed with Tamiya's red-brown (No. XF64), a slightly lighter shade than the Pactra paint.

I made another pass with a flat-black wash, concentrating on details (particularly on the

Filled slot

Mantlet

Fig. 6. To backdate the Tamiya machine-gun emplacement, replace the ball mantlet with a recessed fitting. Joe fitted a Bren machine gun from his spare-parts box.

engine deck), then replicated worn areas by dry-brushing them with gunmetal.

Then I returned my attention to the tracks. I applied gunmetal to the guide horns and to a strip on either side where they meet the road wheels. I applied a flat-black wash to seams between the track plans and dry-brushed the outer edges of the tracks and road wheels with gunmetal.

One last deviation from the kit instructions: Use part B5 for the idler hub; part B4 has too many bolts.

More with less. This is an easy, quick conversion that produces a variant that's instantly recognizable. If you're new to armor modeling, this is an ideal first attempt!

REFERENCES
• Craig, William, *Enemy at the Gates: The Battle for Stalingrad*, Dutton, New York, 1973
• Grove, Eric, *World War II Tanks*, Longmeadow, Stamford, Connecticut, 1987
• Milsom, John, *Russian Tanks, 1900–1970*, Galahad, New York, 1970
• Spielberger, Walter, and Uwe Feist, *Armor on the Eastern Front*, Aero, Fallbrook, California, 1968
• Zaloga, Steven, and James Grandsen, *T-34 in Action*, Squadron/Signal, Carrollton, Texas, 1983

SOURCES
• Epoxy putty: Dr. Microtools, P.O. Box 21585, Columbus, OH 43221
• STZ conversion kit: MB Models, P.O. Box 8241, Charleston, SC 29418
• Styrene sheet and structural shapes: Plastruct, 1020 S. Wallace Place, City of Industry, CA 91748

THE BATTLE OF STALINGRAD

The German Sixth Army laid siege to Stalingrad in August 1942. After the Luftwaffe bombed the city into charred rubble, the Russians dug in for the savage fight that the German soldiers would call Rattenkrieg—War of the Rats.

As Stalingrad fought for its life, tales of heroism became commonplace. Elderly veterans manned the trenches; children operated factory machinery; women braved enemy fire to drag wounded soldiers to safety. Workers died to keep the arms factories running. In August, Stalingrad's Tractor Plant built 400 tanks under artillery fire.

Meanwhile, the Soviet army's hit-and-run tactics whittled away at the German invaders. In November, with winter starting to take hold, a Soviet counterattack surrounded the city. Obedient to Hitler's orders, the German commander Gen. Friedrich von Paulus made no attempt to escape—and his army slowly froze and starved to death. On January 31, 1942, the day after Hitler promoted him to field marshal, Paulus surrendered to Soviet soldiers. A few days later Germany's Sixth Army ceased to exist.

The exact number of casualties will never be known; municipal and military records were destroyed along with everything else. Estimates place the loss of human lives at more than a million.

ACCURIZING ESCI'S 1/35 SCALE LAVS

Getting the "Frog" in shape

Cookie Sewell wasn't satisfied with the profile of Esci's LAVs—so he took matters into his own hands and rebuilt the upper hull to his liking with sheet styrene.

BY COOKIE SEWELL

After a close look at Esci's 1/35 scale LAV-C2, LAV-25, and LAV-TUA TOW launcher, I gave up on building an accurate LAV straight from the box. I decided I would have to correct the entire vehicle profile to get it right. I built Esci's LAV-25 and LAV-TUA TOW launcher, but you can use these techniques on any of the three Esci LAVs. Refer to your kit and instructions as we proceed.

The Esci LAVs have two basic flaws. One, the nose is out of joint. For example, the angles for the two upper nose plates (a total of four panels, two on each side of the nose) are 71 degrees forward, 78 degrees rear—and that's all wrong. The correct angles are 68 degrees forward and 82 degrees rear. The other problem is the suspension, which is so compressed it makes the LAV look like a trolley from a 1930s cartoon.

Suspension and lower hull. Let's start by correcting the suspension, back to front. Cut both rear-axle

Fig. 1 — 10 mm x 62 mm · Tie rod · Drive train · Splash plate · Cut notches

16

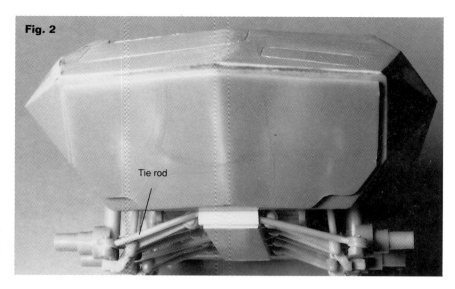

Fig. 2

Tie rod

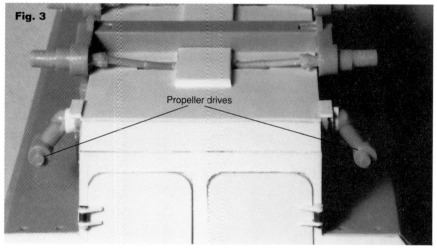

Fig. 3

Propeller drives

housings flush with the hull bottom. Cut a 41 mm x 72 mm plate from .020" sheet styrene to fit the rectangular rear hull bottom, and cut notches in the plate for the rear-wheel drive lines (Fig. 1). Reattach the third axle mount 6 mm from the front edge of the new rear plate, and attach the fourth (front) axle mount 36 mm forward of the rear. The right axles are about a millimeter behind those on the left because of the torsion bars. If you are a real stickler for accuracy, mount the left axles 1.5 mm forward of the right axles: However, you'll have to cut off the mounting tabs, fill the resulting slot, then glue the axle

onto the flat side of the axle box.

To correct the tie rods (parts 25B), trim off the mounting pins of the four axle arms (parts 41B and 42B) and sand the tie-rod mounting pads flush. Glue a 10 mm x 62 mm strip of .080" styrene in the middle of the forward lower hull (Fig. 1). Cut the tie rods to make four 19 mm pieces, each with a pad on the end. Bend each tie rod so one end touches the new center strip, and the pad rests on the top of the axle arm mounting pad (Fig. 2).

Now correct the propeller drives (Fig. 3). Cut off the 90-degree bend in the drive arms (parts 46B and 47B); the long part

will have the propeller gear drive on it. Use scrap plastic to shim the mounts (parts 45B) so the propeller drives project 2 mm from the part 45B pads. Cut the base of the prop drive so the drive is aligned with the axis of the vehicle.

Modify the splash plate (part 15B) according to template G. You will need to scrounge or make two more towing rings, similar to kit part 37B, to mount near the notches. Now complete step 1 of the kit instructions.

Upper hull. Cut the center bulkhead former for the bow section using template B and .040" sheet styrene; test fit it on the inside of the lower hull. Two internal bulkheads, attached to template piece B, support the nose: Template part E fits at the junction of the 68-degree and 82-degree nose angles, and template part F fits on the back edge of template part B (page 18). Cut parts E and F as indicated on the template and glue them to template part B. Glue this assembly on the inside of the forward lower hull.

You can use the kit-supplied part for the rear hull roof plate (part 2E on the APC, part 22C on the TUA), but replace the rest of the upper hull with these pieces of .030" styrene (Fig. 4): two side plates (template A); two upper front cheek pieces (template I); two forward hull deck plates (templates C and D, left and right respectively); and the mid/upper hull deck plate (template part H, Fig. 5). Cut all the pieces before assembling the upper hull, and test fit pieces every step of the way. Reinforce the plate joints with thin strips of sprue glued to the underside of the plates along the mating edges (Fig. 6).

Glue the cheeks (plates I) to

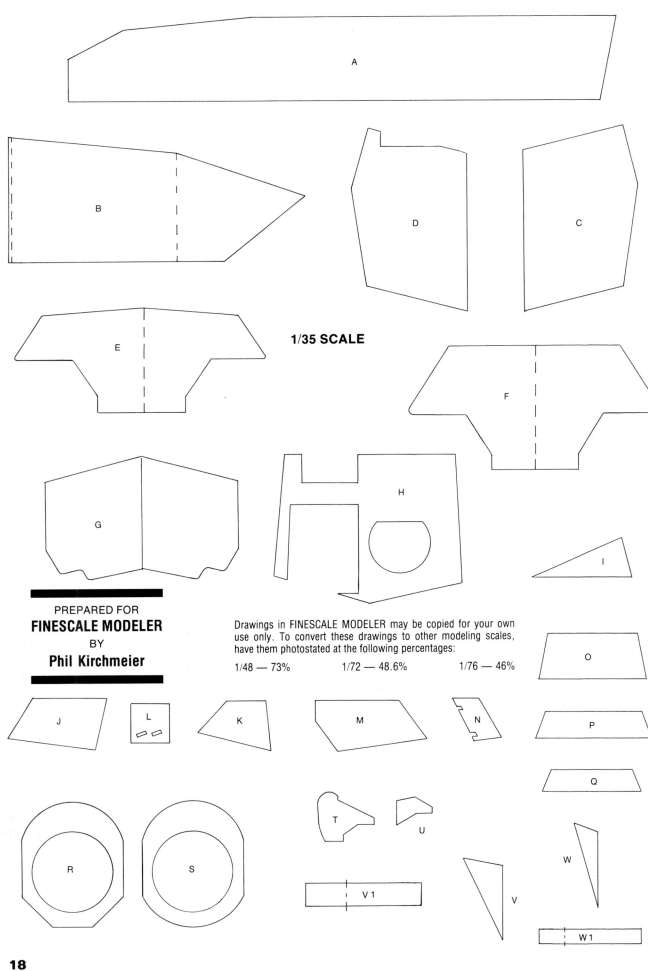

1/35 SCALE

PREPARED FOR
FINESCALE MODELER
BY
Phil Kirchmeier

Drawings in FINESCALE MODELER may be copied for your own use only. To convert these drawings to other modeling scales, have them photostated at the following percentages:

1/48 — 73%   1/72 — 48.6%   1/76 — 46%

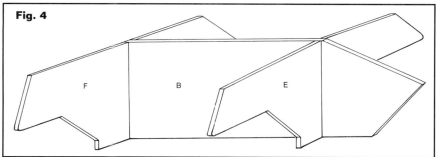

Fig. 4

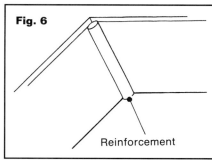

Fig. 6

Reinforcement

Fig. 5

Kit roof

A
H
C
D
I

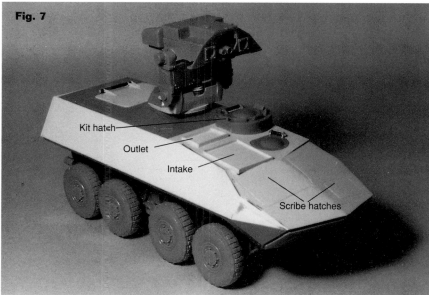

Fig. 7

Kit hatch
Outlet
Intake
Scribe hatches

Note the additional hatch on the TUA, about 51 mm back from the front edge of plate H. Mount plate H behind plates C and D. Glue a strip under the rear edge of the plate as a seat for the kit hull roof, then install the roof. Fill seams with epoxy putty and sand them smooth.

Radiators, hatches, and lights. Now that you've replaced the top half of the hull, you'll have to make new details. Scribe hatches for the engine and the winch bay in the front plates (Fig. 7).

I scratchbuilt a new radiator intake and outlet. The radiator intake is 20 mm wide by 23.5 mm long, and 2.5 mm high overall. Note that it sits level; when viewed in profile, the armor plate descends toward the front and away from the top of the radiator, so the housing looks taller in the front. I used a .5 mm base with .25 mm x .75 mm strip lateral supports and .5 mm rod bars to simulate the grille. The radiator outlet is 12 mm long and 18 mm wide but only 1.5 mm high; it sits deeper in the hull roof (Fig. 7).

Trim the outside lights from the light assemblies. Mount a shrouded night light (U.S. Notek-type) on the left light

the top edges of the lower hull (Fig. 5). Next, glue the sides (plates A) to parts I and the rear bulkhead installed earlier. Install hull plates C and D; make sure they fit the nose, the center former (Fig. 5), the cheek plates (I), and the sides (A).

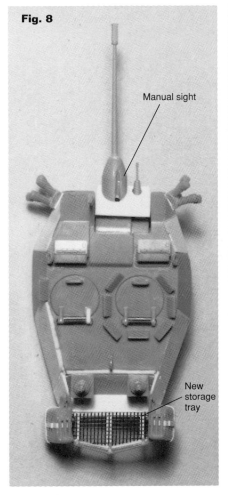

Fig. 8

Manual sight

New storage tray

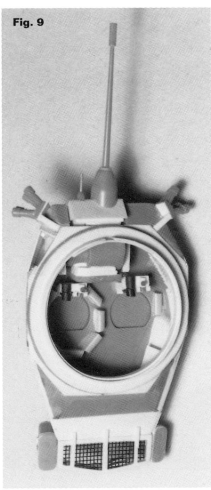

Fig. 9

Fig. 10

Fillet

Grenade tubes

Fig. 11

K

P

N

assembly (it's time to rummage through your scrap box).

Turret and mantlet for the LAV-25. To make a new outer mantlet, cut the mount/shroud from part 21E. (If you have a Tamiya Bradley turret handy, dig it out.) Groove a manual direct sight in the top of the shroud (Fig. 8). Bore a new hole for the coaxial machine gun in the mantlet, too. This aperture is octagonal on the prototype, but you can use a round one, especially with an M240 machine gun barrel and armored jacket (such as is found on the Bradley). The gun barrel extends 52 mm from the back of the mount/shroud to the tip of the muzzle. Set this assembly aside.

Remove the following sections from the top of the turret (part 1E): forward left side panel; rear left side panel; forward right side panel; rear right side panel; and turret stowage tray at turret rear (Fig. 8). Remove the right front side from the lower turret section (part 8E): Start 7.5 mm from the front edge of the turret, cut down at a 90-degree angle, and continue back 11 mm to the joint edge (Fig. 9).

Cut out template parts J, K (make three), L, and M from .030" sheet; cut template parts N (make two) and P from .020" sheet. Use the stowage tray from part 1E as a pattern and cut a new one from .030" sheet. Join parts 1E and 8E, trapping the gun mount (part 22E).

Starting at the right front (Fig. 10), glue template piece L perpendicular to the turret roof; this is the shell ejector plate. Use scrap plastic to fill the rear section of the plate where it joins the roof. Cut the tip of one plate K at a 90-degree angle just behind the leading, top edge of the plate; this mounts on the turret front. Mount another plate K in the opening; this is a movable plate on the real turret. Leave a gap, as if the plate were ajar; put a triangle of sheet at the rear lower edge as a fillet. Mount the rear plate J in place of the previous plate; trim the remaining turret section to receive the new plate.

On the left side (Fig. 11), trim the remaining section to receive the forward plate K. Plate M must be trimmed to fit. Fill the joints and sand them smooth.

Cement the guard wings (plates N) to plate P, and mount the stowage tray on the edge of plate P with strip styrene (Fig. 11). Note that some LAV-25s have an extra pair of jerry cans on the sides of the turret rack; this may help you when aligning the stowage bin. I recommend replacing the kit parts with either Tamiya or Italeri jerry cans.

Mount the new gun mantlet. Correct the smoke grenade launchers: Trim the tabs from the backs of parts 17E and mount the grenade tubes (parts 14B) on a triangle of scrap plastic on the lower turret front (Fig. 10). To add an M60 machine gun mount in front of the commander's hatch (right side), bend an .080" rod in a 13-mm-diameter circle, glue a small tube at the top of the circle to mount the machine gun, and use scrap rod as the mount base. Use either Tamiya or Italeri's M60.

Turret for the TUA. The commander's cupola (part 5C) mounts in the same place, but if you want an open hatch you should trace the outline of the part on the new roof and cut a hole about 1.5 mm inside the outline (Fig. 12).

The "hammerhead" launcher

Fig. 12

Cheeks

Turret base

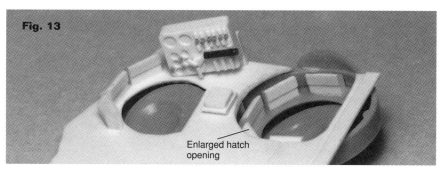

Fig. 13

Enlarged hatch opening

Fig. 14

New launcher base

Gunner's cupola

Loader's hatch

is the key assembly on the TUA: Use the kit-supplied launcher (assembly 3D), as well as kit assemblies G, K, and J. Remember, if

you glue the umbilical cable (part 38C) the launcher won't move. The gunner's cupola and hatch (parts 6C and 15C) are fine, but

Fig. 15

Fig. 16

the base plate (part 14C) must be redone (Fig. 13). Cut two pieces of .040" sheet using templates R and S. Part R is the top, part 15C cements to it, and part S is the new cupola base (Fig. 14).

Don't bother using kit assemblies E and F. Use .040" sheet to make two pieces from template T. Laminate three pieces of .040" to each piece, but only along the rounded forward portion.

You can join these to part 16C, or make a new piece from .030" sheet. Glue the new cheek pieces (template parts T3) to part 16C. Cut two parts from .030" sheet according to template U. Each template part U mounts inside the launcher assembly and forms a brace with a flat pad that mounts on part 15C (Fig. 13). The new launcher base mounts around the front edge of the gunner's cupola (Fig. 14).

On the actual launcher there are hydraulic rams on either side of the umbilical cable, but I left these off so I could pose the launcher.

Rear details of the TUA. The side guards (parts 34C and 35C)

are okay, but mount them 14 mm from the rear of the roof.

One of parts 31C mounts over the holes for the grab handle (part 11B) on the left hull, flush with the top of the hull with its lower rear corner touching the rear (Fig. 15). Cut the tab off the top of part 30C, fill, then put it in the same spot as 31C but on the right side of the hull (Fig. 16).

You need to replace parts 18C and 19C, but don't discard them yet. From .020" sheet, make two pieces from template V and four pieces from template W. Cut template V1 from .030" sheet and attach it to template pieces V as indicated (Fig. 17). Use .030" sheet for template W1; make two.

Assemble templates W and W1 as indicated. Glue the V assembly to the left side of the hull with its rear edge 26 mm from the rear of the roof (Fig. 15); it should be centered under the hole in part 34C. Mount the W assemblies 8 mm from the rear of the roof forward of part 31C and its counterpart, 30C (Figs. 16 and 17).

Mount the other part 31C on the right of the hull, 39 mm from the rear (Fig. 16). Cut off the mount of part 18C and center it on top of assembly V (Fig. 15). Remove the mount (top) of part 19C and glue the mount atop the assembly W (Fig. 15).

Put part 21C 8 mm from the rear and 9.5 mm from the right edge of the roof. Now run a 4 mm x 7 mm x 1.5 mm strip of plastic from the edge of the roof through the hole in kit part part 35C (Fig. 16). Mount kit part 20C at the end of this strip (Fig. 16); part 20C's other edge touches the opening for the loader's hatch. (Note: The "blade" of the mount travels parallel to the center line of the vehicle, rather than perpendicular to it as shown in the kit directions.)

Now add rubber bumpers and mounts to the new versions of parts 18C, 19C, 20C, and 21C, using strip styrene and 1 mm slices of 2 mm rod to simulate rubber pads. Add triangles (12 mm base, 5 mm sides) of .030" sheet to kit assemblies G and J along the ridges just under the top hinges on the outside of each part. These parts rest on mounts 18C and 20C; adjust to fit. Use scrap for two small bumpers under the rear of the launcher assembly. The launcher head rests on these when lowered for travel.

GENERAL MOTORS LAV-25 AND LAV-AT (TUA)

General Motors of Canada, Diesel Division, produced the first LAVs in early 1979, the MOWAG Piranha six-wheeled LAV (light armored vehicle) for Canadian armed forces. The U.S. Army and Marine Corps selected an eight-wheeled variant for rapid-deployment forces.

The vanguard land forces of Operation Desert Storm came equipped with LAVs. By their nature, LAVs are front-line weapons: they can be air dropped, they have a top speed of 62 mph, and they provide protection against small arms fire.

The LAV-25 is 25' long, 8'2" wide, 8'10" tall (or 8'5" without the pintle mount), and weighs 24,100 pounds in combat. Its main weapon is an M242 Bushmaster 25 mm automatic cannon. The LAV-25 mounts two 7.62 mm machine guns (M240 and M60E3) and two M257 smoke grenade launchers, and it carries a crew of nine.

The LAV-AT (antitank or TUA) is taller (10'3") and heavier (27,650 pounds loaded). It mounts an M901A1 TOW II missile launcher as well as an M60E3 machine gun and two M257 smoke grenade launchers. The LAV-AT carries a crew of four.

LAVs can cross a 6'9"-wide trench and climb grades as steep as 60 percent. And they're amphibious: Two propellers generate a swimming speed of 6 mph. (In a landlocked operation the propellers can be removed.) A 275 hp Detroit Diesel and a five speed Allison transmission power four rear drive wheels (eight-wheel drive is optional). With an independent suspension and power-assisted brakes and steering, driving an LAV is like driving a heavy-duty truck. Photos courtesy of General Motors of Canada.

SOURCE
• Sheet styrene: Evergreen Scale Models, 12808 N. E. 125th Way, Kirkland, WA 98034

BUILDING AN IRAQI T-62M IN 1/35 SCALE

Converting and accurizing Tamiya's Soviet tank

Left: We know a lot more about the Soviet-built T-62 than we did when Tamiya released its 1/35 scale kit in 1978. Cookie's improvements show the difference.

Below left: Iraqi tanks were no match for American firepower in Desert Storm—but this Iraqi T-62 still looks menacing.

BY COOKIE SEWELL

In the days before Soviet glasnost lifted the Iron Curtain, Tamiya released its 1/35 scale T-62A (kit No. 35108) and armor modelers rejoiced. It was 1978, and Tamiya's kit was the only modern Soviet tank available. Today, with information and aftermarket conversion and detail sets available in abundance, it's much easier to build a Soviet tank such as my Iraqi T-62M.

If you like simply building straight from the box—and there's nothing wrong with that!—MB Models kit No. 1065 features a T-62M turret and resin skirts. It's a goof-proof conversion designed for the Tamiya kit.

Another option—even more accurate, but also more ambitious—is to buy a new turret and scratchbuild other elements of the conversion. I used Chesapeake Model Designs' resin turret (No. CMD-006) plus parts from the following kits: DML's T-72M (No. 3502, but their T-72M2 No. 3501 also works), Lindberg's T-55 (No. 76001); and Esci's T-55 (No. 5044).

First cuts. Slice off the suspension arms from the hull; be careful, because you'll want to reuse them.

Cut out the engine deck with a razor saw.

Figure 1 shows how I reshaped the hull sides and rear. Measure 2 mm down from the rear of the upper hull, draw a guideline to the turret-race plate, and trim away this portion of the hull to angle the engine deck. Saw off the end of the hull, from 6 mm behind where the rear left suspension arm meets the hull bottom and perpendicular to the hull top. Cut away the fenders between the tips and the tails, except for the exhaust. Figure 2 shows what's left.

To restore the hull length, cut new rear sides and a lower back

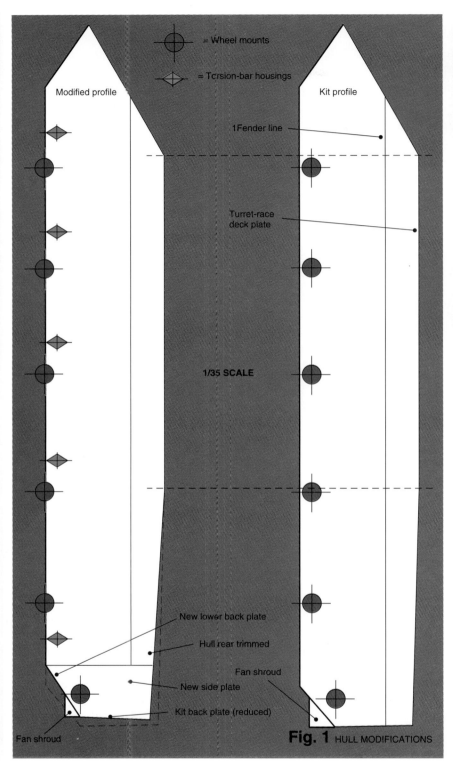

= Wheel mounts

= Torsion-bar housings

Modified profile

Kit profile

1Fender line

Turret-race deck plate

1/35 SCALE

New lower back plate

Hull rear trimmed

Fan shroud

New side plate

Kit back plate (reduced)

Fan shroud

Fig. 1 HULL MODIFICATIONS

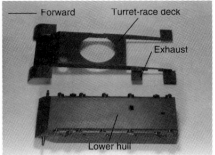

Forward

Turret-race deck

Exhaust

Lower hull

Fig. 2. Here's what's left of the Tamiya hull after Cookie has made his cut.

Fan shroud

Fig. 3. The fan shroud is just as wide as it was before, but not as tall.

the upper hull in place, test fit the plates, then glue them firmly in place.

Drive wheels, suspension, and a new bottom. I swiped drive-wheel mounts from an Esci T-55 kit and trimmed their bolt rings down, Fig. 4. You can easily scratchbuild them: Cut circles 17 mm wide from .040" sheet. Place the center of the circle 14 mm from the top of the lower-hull rear and 8 mm aft of where the new side plate joins the hull, Fig. 1. After gluing it in place, trim the new rear hull to match the profile of the new mount. You'll need small shims at the front of the new side plates to match the circle, Fig. 4.

Trim the kit's final-drive sumps to match the new profile— for me this took patience, a razor saw, and a string of earthy, persuasive Anglo-Dutch phrases.

I glued .010" sheet to the bottom of the hull, adding a cutout for the driver's escape hatch, torsion-bar housings 6 mm in

plate from .040" sheet styrene to match the modified area of Fig. 1. Use the kit's back plate, but trim off its mounting tabs and cut it to fit the new rear hull profile. Carefully slice off back plate details with a razor blade and fill holes with Squadron Green Stuff putty. Trim the fan shroud to 4 mm tall, but keep it the same width. Use putty to form the fan shroud on the lower back plate, Fig. 3. Tape

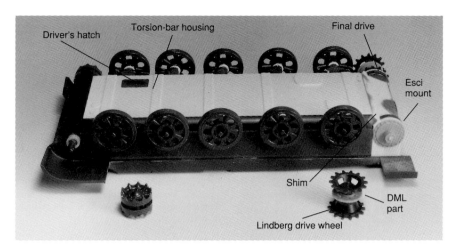

Driver's hatch Torsion-bar housing Final drive

Esci mount

Shim

DML part

Lindberg drive wheel

Fig. 4 (left). Now that the lower hull is back together, fit the drive-wheel mount, the final-drive housing, and the drive wheel. Lower-hull details are made from .020" sheet styrene.

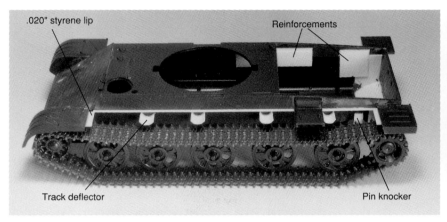

.020" styrene lip Reinforcements

Track deflector Pin knocker

Grandt Line bolt

Modified hub

Fig. 5. The .020" styrene lip will mount the fenders. The close-up shows a modified T-55 driver.

width made from .020" sheet, as well as other minor details.

Now glue the suspension arms to restore them to the correct angle and give the model the right height. Figure 1 shows the positions of the wheel mounts and torsion-bar housings.

Build a small jig from .040" sheet styrene and two .040" strips (one on each end of the sheet). Set the hull on this jig and reattach the arms so the lower end of the arm touches the jig. If you damaged the kit arms when removing them you can replace them with Esci T-55 arms.

Link the shock absorbers to the front and rear arms and attach a track-pin knocker to the hull rear, 12 mm forward from the

driver mount, Fig. 5. (The early T-62s used loose pins that came out periodically; this knocked them back in place.) The knocker is a 3 mm x 6 mm strip of .040" styrene, sanded to a roof shape with a center ridge. I also made track deflectors from .020" sheet.

The wheels are next. I reshaped the spokes with a file, then fitted .020" styrene washer shims behind the wheels and mounted them, Fig. 4.

Tracks. If you want to stick with the kit tracks, install them later. I preferred to use the track from DML's T-72M, but it wouldn't fit the Tamiya drive wheels. You could just mount the DML sprockets, but I substituted a pair from Lindberg's T-55, grinding a ring in

them and adding Grandt Line styrene bolts, Fig. 5. Using the center disk from the DML wheel helped improve the fit of the tracks, Fig. 4.

The DML track needs some adjustment. Soak it in hot water to get the right sag in the top run before you install it. I decided to leave off the outer row of road wheels to make painting easier, Fig. 5.

Once the wheels and tracks were on, I added an .020" styrene lip around the fender openings for a fender mount, Fig. 5. I also glued .040" scraps inside the engine-bay front to reinforce the hull.

Carefully slice all details from the glacis (you'll reuse many of them), fill openings in that plate,

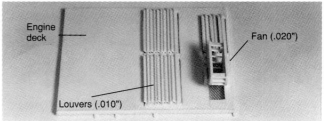

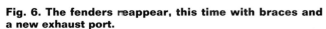

Fig. 6. The fenders reappear, this time with braces and a new exhaust port.

Fig. 7. Aluminum screen makes the engine deck look better, but creates more work. Now that you can see through the screen, you have to build something to look at!

and glue the upper and lower hulls together.

Fenders and engine deck. Make new fenders from .030" sheet, Fig. 6. Drill .030" holes 6 mm apart and 4 mm in from the edge to replicate fender drain holes. The left fender passes under the exhaust and becomes the bottom of that aperture.

Make a lip from .010" strip and glue it on the outside edge of the fenders. Cut braces from .020" sheet, and an exhaust port from .010" sheet. Cut a new engine deck from .040" sheet and replicated the screening with Scale Structures diamond-pattern aluminum mesh and .010" trim, Fig. 7.

The louvers are also .010" strip, Fig. 7; each looks like a lowercase "h" with the long side on top and the open part facing the rear. There are five under each radiator screen and three under the transmission radiator screen. To detail the remaining screen I made a dummy fan structure from .020" scraps.

Hull details. Most of the parts on the engine deck have been scratchbuilt. However, I shaped a portion of the kit's engine deck with a motor tool and dental burr to replicate the fan's fording cover, Fig. 8. Additionally, I cut radiator fording covers from the kit's engine deck, doubling their thickness with .040" strip. The covers' hinges are made of rod and strip scraps.

Use the kit's stowage box lids and fronts, but add two new boxes. One, behind the slanted box on the left rear, contains a flapper valve that covers the exhaust port during fording. The other is an Iraqi add-on located forward of the rammer stowage bin amidships on the left, Fig. 9. Make them from .020" sheet.

I made box tie-downs from scrap plastic and Grandt Line bolts, but you can take a shortcut by using tie-downs from On The Mark's T-54/55 photoetched brass detail set (No. TMP3510).

Add a front-fender return spring and lock and an eyelet for the lock; make them from .020" rod and strip. Install an oil tank above the exhaust, a shovel behind the rammer bin, and a horn at the front of the left sponson just behind the fender brace, Fig. 9. Tow cable U-bolt and fuel tank mounts go on the right side.

Fuel tanks and glacis plates. Like other Soviet tanks, the T-62 uses a self-balancing closed-loop fuel system. There are two feeds to the engine, and the three tanks are interconnected, Fig. 9. Drill two .030" holes in the fuel tanks to accept the lines; carefully slice off the handle at the tapered end with a razor blade and move it right of center. Make filling and cleanout plugs from plastic scraps.

Make a headlight brush guard from three pieces of .040" sheet, cut to shape, trimmed, and sanded, Fig. 10. Glue the lights in

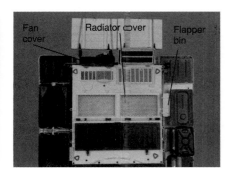

Fig. 8. These fording covers don't come with the kit, but they're not hard to make.

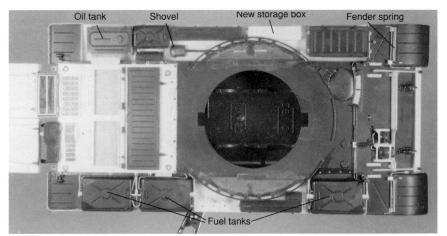

Fig. 9. Most of these stowage boxes are supplied in the kit. Cookie added one of these boxes and dressed up the front fenders with easy-to-model return springs.

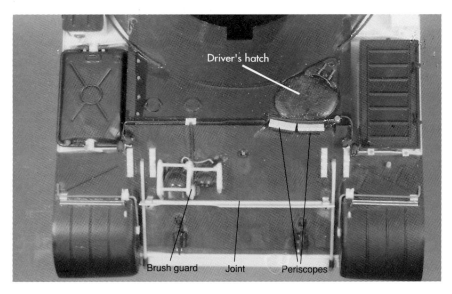

Fig. 10. Details make the difference up front, too.

Fig. 11. Finishing touches at the hull rear. Iraqi tankers replaced Soviet spare-fuel cans at the back with wood boxes.

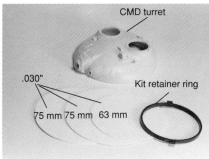

Fig. 12. The bottom of Chesapeake Model designs' resin turret is hollow—these sheet-styrene disks fill the void.

place and connect the frame with .030" rod. You can cut a splash board from .010" sheet; attach .010" strip to give it a look of stamped metal.

Replicate the glacis-plate joint with an .030" x .005" sheet, then attach tow hooks. Add plow mounts using sections of .010" rod instead of bolts.

Detail the driver's periscopes with scrap, too. Contrary to the kit, the driver's hatch is domed: I got a second T-62 hatch from my spare parts, cut off its mount, sanded it down around the edges, and glued it on top of the first one. A generous coat of Testor's liquid cement, stippled with a stubby old paintbrush, gave it a rough, cast look.

Back to the back. Make a new fan-boss cover and a manual-starter cover from .030" styrene, Fig. 11. I added mounts for a re-covery beam, two T-72 track links with tie-downs, and moved the tow hooks.

Some Iraqi tanks retain the fuel-drum mounts for extra stow-age; so did I, adding two boxes made from .030" sheet. I repli-cated wood grain by scraping the boxes with a razor saw, then mounted them with waxed cord for rope, Fig. 11.

Corrected turret and fittings. Because I used CMD's turret, I had to make a turret base from .030" sheet styrene, Fig. 12. Here's how to do it:

Cut the retainer ring (with tabs) from the kit turret base. Then cut three disks, two 75 mm in diameter and one 63 mm in diameter, from .030" sheet. Lam-inate the 75 mm disks to build an .060" plate to fill the base of the CMD turret, then glue on the 63 mm disk to replicate the T-62's

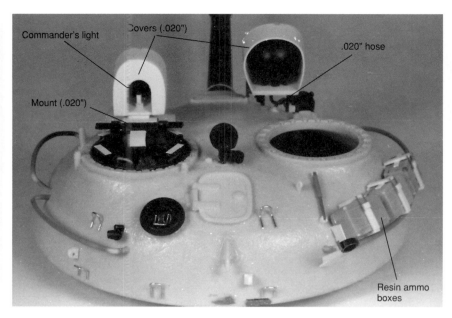

Commander's light

Covers (.020")

.020" hose

Mount (.020")

Resin ammo boxes

Fig. 13. Looking at the searchlights from behind shows how Cookie mounted them. He also cast the ammo boxes in resin.

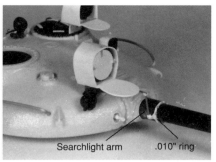

Searchlight arm　　**.010" ring**

Fig. 14. Simple hinges hold the light-cover lids; the arm and its mount are nifty extras.

2,200 mm turret race and 25 mm standoff (read "daylight") under the turret.

Use the kit's searchlight, but thin the main light mounts with a file and discard the base; cut off the tabs on top. Super glue the thinned mounts to the turret, then file them level and complete the mount with .020" sheet; glue it to the top of the swivel mounts, Fig. 13.

I made a searchlight cover from .020" sheet; the cover base is 10 mm x 10 mm. I curved a 10 mm-wide strip of .020" sheet by pulling it over the edge of a table. Two .020" shims on the sides hold the ring's shape. When the glue dried I drilled an .060" hole in the center of the mount and into the light.

I cut a cover lid from .020" sheet to match the new shape, added a hinge of .020" rod, then installed the light, Fig. 14. Finally, I modeled a power cable with .020" Verlinden neoprene hose, running it from the CMD power block to the center hole underneath the light mount, Fig. 13.

The commander's light is modified in the same way as the main light, except that it has a back with a U-shaped notch in it. The commander's-light base is 9.55 mm x 9.5 mm, but the wrapped cover tapers to 7.55 mm.

I detailed the Tamiya gun barrel with an .010" ring for a searchlight-arm mount at the joint near the rear, Fig. 14, and detailed it with 10 Grandt Line bolts and a modified Grandt Line turnbuckle for the articulated arm.

I cast extra ammo boxes in resin (when you use a lot of Soviet parts as I do, it makes sense) and mounted them on the right side, Fig. 13. I made other details from brass wire, styrene, and resin.

Cupola, gun, and skirts. I recommend several changes to the loader's cupola and the 12.7 mm machine gun, Fig. 15. Cut off the balance springs and glue the

Balance springs

.020"

Fig. 15. A styrene ring under the loader's hatch lets the gun traverse.

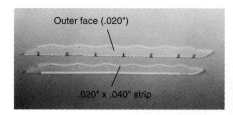

Outer face (.020")

.020" x .040" strip

Fig. 16. Chinese skirts: T-62 fender skirts are like those of China's Type 69 tank.

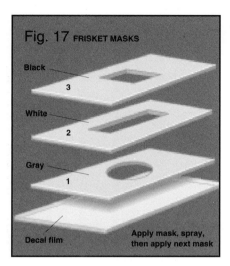

Fig. 17 FRISKET MASKS

Black — 3

White — 2

Gray — 1

Decal film

Apply mask, spray, then apply next mask

cradle and gun together. I made balance spring housings from styrene strip and rod and Contrail styrene tubing. Use scraps for details such as locks and pins as well as the firing trigger on the left and the charging handle under the receiver; fill in the housing on top of the receiver. I detailed the hatch, cleaned up its hinges, and added bump stops. Attaching an .020" styrene ring under the loader's hatch allowed the gun to traverse.

I wanted to capture the not-quite-thick-enough look of the real tank's fiberglass skirts: I made them from .020" sheet, .020" rod, .010" x .030" strip, and detailed them with Grandt Line bolts, Fig. 16. Gluing .020" x .040" strip to the insides, .030" below the top of the skirt, provided a mount.

Paint and markings. I airbrushed Humbrol F94 Eighth Army sand over a base coat of Testor's Modelmaster SAC bomber tan, then applied a black wash to the recesses and a rust wash to the raised details (the latter is a fancy touch on sand-colored vehicles).

The tracks are painted Floquil boxcar red, Floquil grime, and finally a topcoat of Rub 'n Buff silver leaf. The gun barrel's bore exhaust is Floquil signal yellow with a Floquil reefer white stripe; the numbers and Iraqi flags came from my DML kit's decal sheet.

I made regimental insignia using frisket paper masks (available at art supply stores) and clear decal film, Fig. 17. Apply a circle mask to the decal film and spray it Floquil medium gull gray. Mask a rectangle and spray it reefer white, then mask a smaller rectangle in the center and spray Floquil engine black.

After removing the frisket paper I drew the Arabic "QX" (for Qadisiyah Saddam or Saddam's Holy Battle) with an extra-fine-tip alcohol marker. My tank is from the Second Regiment, Sixth Brigade, Third Saladin Armored Division.

New tricks for an old tank. Tamiya's T-62 is an old kit, but it's still receptive to new tricks. Even if you buy three kits—a T-62A, a T-55, and a conversion set—you'll probably only spend about $50. And that's considerably less than you would pay for just one high-tech kit!

T-62 MAIN BATTLE TANK

The Soviet T-62 developed from the earlier T-54 and T-55 series in the late 1950s. It entered production in 1961 and made its public debut in a 1965 Moscow parade. Soviet production of the T-62 ceased in 1975, by which time 20,000 had been built. Another 1,500 were built for export in Czechoslovakia between 1973 and 1978.

The design didn't change much until 1972, when the T62M went into production. The new model differed mainly in its turret shape and the replacement of a fixed loader's hatch with a rotating cupola that mounted a DShKM 12.7mm antiaircraft machine gun, the latter correcting a serious omission (earlier models had no antiaircraft armament). Later updates included appliqué armor, a laser range finder, and a ballistic computer.

The T-62 lacked popularity outside of the Soviet Union. Two of the main customers were Syria and Iraq, buying 1,000 and 1,400, respectively. Iraq solved the problem of the missing antiaircraft gun by adding a hasty copy of the T-54/T-55M cupola to its T-62s. Another prominent Iraqi alteration was the installation of fiberglass skirts such as those found on the Chinese Type 69.

Iraq issued its first T-62s to elite formations and the Republican Guard; later the tank became a regular-army weapon. Most Iraqi T-62s were destroyed in Operation Desert Storm.

SOURCES
• Photoetched detail parts: On the Mark Models, P.O. 663, Louisville, CO 80027
• Scale structures aluminum screening: JAKS Industries, P.O. Box 1421, 913 Eighth St., Golden, CO 80402
• Sheet, tube, and rod styrene: Evergreen Scale Models, 12808 N. E. 125th Way, Kirkland, WA 98034
• Styrene detailing bolts: Grandt Line Products, Inc., 1040B Shary Court, Concord, CA 94518
• Clear decal film: ATP/Airliners America, 3014 Abelia Court, San Jose, CA 95121
• T-62M conversion kit: MB Models, P.O. Box 8241, Festival Center, Charleston, SC 29418
• T-62M turret conversion: Chesapeake Model Designs, Box 393, Monkton, MD 21111
• Contrail styrene rod and tubing: Available from Imported Specialties, 3655 Sullivant Ave., Columbus, OH 43228
• Neoprene hose: Verlinden Productions, 811 Lone Star Drive, Lone Star Industrial Park, O'Fallon, MO 63366

REFERENCES
• Englehart, Tony, and Pat Foran, *Sword in the Sand*, Concord Publishing, Hong Kong, 1991
• Gilbert, Ed, and Allen Swan, *T-62*, Full Detail Publishing, Katy, Texas, 1989

MODEL APPLIQUÉ ARMOR PLATE IN 1/35 SCALE

Dressing up for D-Day

To emphasize the difference between field- and factory-applied armor Ed modeled both early and late Shermans being prepared for Operation Overlord at an ordnance repair unit. The old M4A1 is being reworked and has been stripped of its tracks and machine guns. A welder has just finished adding the last appliqué plate. In the background, a new M4A3 with factory-installed appliqué and track grousers is prepared for issue.

BY ED GILBERT

One of the most distinctive features of Sherman tanks used in World War Two was appliqué armor, steel plates welded on the outside of the hull and turret. Many of the Shermans lost at El Alamein were destroyed when shells penetrated the hull and ex-ploded ammunition stored inside. Other weak spots in the Sherman's skin were raised hoods over the driver's and hull gunner's heads and the right front face of the turret, where armor was thinner to make room for the gun controls.

The Army Ordnance Department was desperate for tanks and decided to beef up these weak spots by adding external armor plates instead of stopping production while redesigning the tank. Vehicles already in service would have the additional armor added by maintenance units in the field. By June 1944, all the older tanks in England and the Pacific had been fitted with appliqué armor, but a few Shermans soldiered on

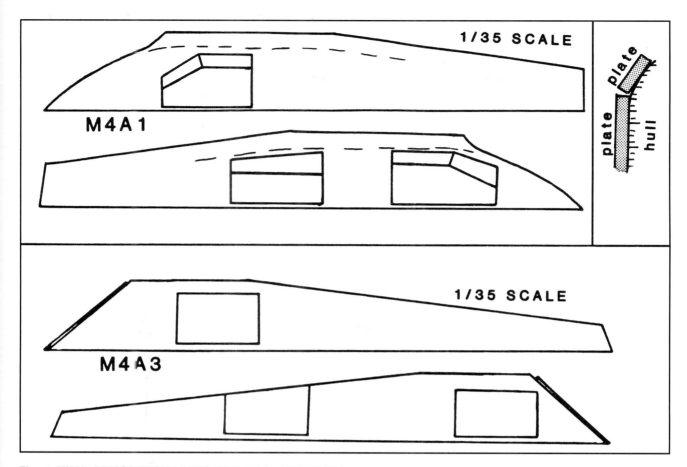

Fig. 1. HULL ARMOF TEMPLATES FOR M4A1 AND M4A3

until the end of the war in Italy without the added protection.

Shermans with HVSS suspension or armed w th 76 mm or 105 mm guns dicn't have the added armor. The Testor/Italeri or Revell M4A1 kits therefore wouldn't need additional armor. However, by putting the Tamiya turret on a Testor hull, a ate production M4A1 with a 75 mm gun can be modeled. Many of these had factory-installed plates. Most British Fireflies also had a more complicated appliqué arrangement.

Good kits of the Sherman are available, but most don't feature appliqué armor. Tamiya's M4A3 (No. MM222A) includes three optional hull plates, but they're thin and not realistic. No kit includes turret plates.

I built two models—a late version M4A3 with appliqué plates added at the factory and an older M4AI being fitted with plates by a maintenance unit. I used the Tamiya M4A3 and Nichimo M4A1 (No. SR3503). The Nichimo kit is the only 1/36 scale early-production Sherman available.

Production-line armor on an M4A3. Appliqué armor added at the factory frequently had rounded corners, was neatly welded to the vehicle, and had the weld joint smoothed before the tank was painted. Official specifications called for 1"-thick plates on the hull and turret face.

To simulate this in 1/35 scale, I used Evergreen .030" plastic sheet because it's flexible enough

to bend easily around the compound curve of the turret face (I originally used sheet plastic from an industrial supplier, but it was brittle). Hull side plate templates are provided for the M4A3 and M4A1, Fig. 1.

For plates with rounded corners, first trim the plates square, then round the corners. Glue the plates in position and allow them to dry thoroughly.

To simulate the weld bead I used a two-part epoxy putty. Filler putty is too soft and grainy and hardens too quickly. I rolled out a thin thread of putty, about the same diameter as the thickness of the plate, laid the thread into the angle between the hull and the plate, and pressed it in with my finger, Fig. 2. If the thread is too

Fig. 2. A thread of putty is pressed into the angle between the hull and side plate on this production-line armor. There is no bead along the lower edge of the plate.

big, use a sharp knife to carefully scrape away the extra, and press again. I didn't worry about fingerprints in the putty—they simulate the marks left by a power grinder. The plates weren't welded along the bottom edge, so I didn't add a bead there.

The turret armor is harder to model. I cut a plate from .030" plastic (for the Nichimo kit, make a slightly larger plate, cutting along the dashed line).

Some tanks had turret appliqué made of two plates. For these versions, scribe along the dotted line shown on the template. Glue the inboard edge parallel to the edge of the gun mount opening, Fig. 3.

When the first joint was dry, I coated the back of the plate with liquid glue and pressed it tightly to the turret, bending it to fit. I positioned clamps to hold all the edges tight, and allowed it to dry. Make the fit as good as possible along the upper edges of the plate.

If you have trouble getting the bottom edge to fit, wait until the glue is dry, then gently heat the plastic with a soldering iron and press it into place until it cools and hardens. I followed the same technique used on the hull plates to add the weld beads, making a flat bead in the scribed line.

Field shop armor on an M4A1. Armor fitted by field units was seldom elegant. Often the plates were cut from wrecked or captured vehicles, or from large plates obtained from a rolling mill. Edges of the plates were left rough from the cutting torch, and the weld beads were not usually ground smooth. Although harder to model, this type of armor is interesting because of the textural details.

Templates for this type of armor are also provided in Fig. 1. The side plates on the M4A1 consisted of several flat sections arranged to follow the curve of the hull as much as possible, Fig. 4.

To simulate the rough edge left by a cutting torch, I cut small, closely spaced nicks into the bottom edge of each plate with a triangular file, Fig. 5. I touched up the rough edges with fine sandpaper just enough to knock off the plastic whiskers. Only the bottom edge needs to be sanded because the other sides will be covered by weld beads.

I made a thread of putty, pressed it into the joint just enough to make it stick, and trimmed off any extra. Then using a pencil with the lead sanded to a flat, chisel-like edge, I prodded the putty into a series of small lumps, Fig. 6. I alternated pushing at a slight angle, first from one side, then the other. It took practice to get the feel of the technique.

When the putty hardens, it will look too lumpy—don't worry. Paint will fill in the low spots slightly, smoothing out the texture of the weld bead.

To simulate fresh steel, I brushed the appliqué plates with the gummy residue of pigment left after pouring off the solvent

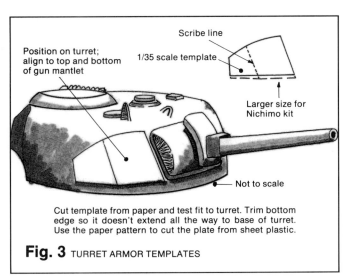

Position on turret; align to top and bottom of gun mantlet

Scribe line

1/35 scale template

Larger size for Nichimo kit

Not to scale

Cut template from paper and test fit to turret. Trim bottom edge so it doesn't extend all the way to base of turret. Use the paper pattern to cut the plate from sheet plastic.

Fig. 3 TURRET ARMOR TEMPLATES

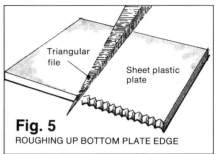

Fig. 5
ROUGHING UP BOTTOM PLATE EDGE

Fig. 4. Ed's M4A1 with new sectioned appliqué armor plate in place. Note the rough cut on the bottom edges simulating torch-cut metal.

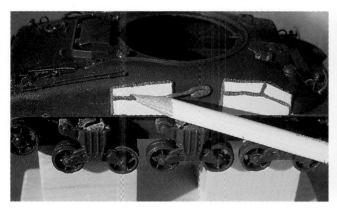

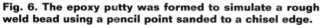

Fig. 6. The epoxy putty was formed to simulate a rough weld bead using a pencil point sanded to a chisel edge.

Fig. 7. Once painted and weathered, the plastic and putty look like welded rolled steel.

from a bottle of Model Master Steel. I brushed each plate at a different angle, so that the texture would replicate the lined appearance of rolled steel plate. Plate edges and the surrounding tank hull were dry-brushed with flat black to simulate scorching by the welder's torch, Fig. 7. The fresh weld beads were highlighted by dry-brushing with Model Master Chrome Silver, followed by a light dry-brushing with metallic blue.

REFERENCES
• Gilbert, Ed, "Appliqué Armor on the M4 Sherman Tank," IPMS/U. S. A. *Quarterly*, Vol. 22, 1986
• Hunnicutt, R. P., *Sherman—A History of the American Medium Tank*, Presidio Press, Novato, California, 1978

MODELING A PHÄNOMEN GRANIT 1500

An easy conversion based on Italeri's 1/35 scale Horch KFZ 15

Simple scratchbuilding techniques and masterful painting are key elements in Gérard's easy-to-do conversion to model this World War Two German ambulance.

BY GÉRARD DEYGAS

World War Two German military vehicles were notable for diversity and distinctive design. This variety intrigues modelers looking for something new to build. Searching for an unusual subject, I came upon the Phänomen Granit 1500 ambulance. It's hard to find pictures of this 1½-ton truck—and it's impossible to find a model kit of the Granit. So I decided to build one myself.

Building supplies. My Phänomen Granit is a conversion of Italeri's 1/35 scale Horch KFZ 15 (kit No. 215). Most of the body is rebuilt. To do this conversion you'll need the following tools and supplies:

- sheet styrene (.020" and .010")
- epoxy filler putty
- needle-shaped and flat emery boards
- an X-acto knife (with a No. 6 blade)
- a metal ruler (to make straight cuts)
- a ⅛"-thick sheet of balsa wood
- clear plastic (for the windows)

Alterations to the Italeri chassis. Though the Italeri Horch KFZ 15 is a good kit, it's going to be

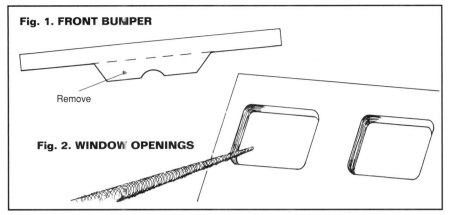

Fig. 1. FRONT BUMPER

Remove

Fig. 2. WINDOW OPENINGS

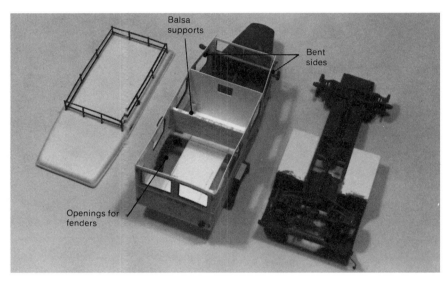

Balsa supports

Bent sides

Openings for fenders

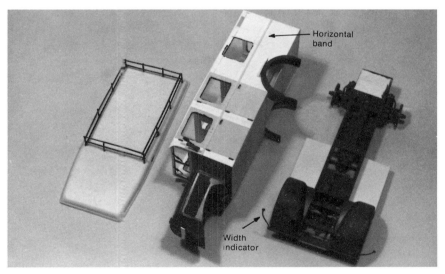

Horizontal band

Width indicator

(Upper) Fig. 3. Gérard used pieces of balsa wood to reinforce the body assembly. This photo shows the underside of the chassis. Don't forget to leave room in the floor for the rear fenders! (Lower) Fig. 4. The width indicators help a driver to avoid bending his fenders. A strip of .010" styrene replicates side trim.

severely modified to build the Granit. Begin by removing the front and rear floorboards, the axles and the supports for the spare tires, supports for the headlights, the air intakes on the hood, and the bars covering the radiator (stretched-sprue bars, arranged in a horizontal pattern, will replace the Horch's vertical bars).

All the holes on the upper part of the front fenders must be filled; these holes were intended for the headlights, emblem of the division, and other features of the Horch KFZ 15. Also, fill the holes for the tow hooks on the front.

I removed the mud flaps on the rear fenders and replaced them with paper, cut to a more accurate shape. Up front, cut off the flange on the lower part of the front bumper, leaving only a horizontal bar (Fig. 1).

Cut the front running boards from sheet styrene, according to the templates on page 39 (these are template pieces 12 and 13). Again, note that the pieces for the body are .020" sheet styrene, the doors .010".

The steering, suspension, universal joints, and gearbox need no modification. Keep all the interior details of the cab: gear lever, pedals, steering wheel, and dashboard. **Seats.** The seats need improving. I covered them with tissue soaked in a mixture of wood glue and water, then shaped them. After the seat covers dried (5–6 hours), I cut away excess material. Then I painted them burnt sienna, followed by a black wash. When the paint dries, the surface of the seats can be buffed to a satin gloss that has the look of leather. You can replicate tears or splits in the seat covers by slicing them with an X-acto knife.

Body. Cut the pieces for the sides and rear of the truck body (pieces 2, 3, and 4) and the rear wall of the driver's cab (piece 14). Pieces 2 and 3 are bent slightly (Fig. 3) to meet the Italeri motor hood (part 19 in the Italeri kit); scribe them according to the dotted line on the template, then test fit with the cab wall in place.

Now cut the window openings, using the needle-shaped emery file to round the corners (Fig. 2). Next, assemble the body. I reinforced this assembly with balsa-wood supports (Fig. 3). Cut the styrene piece for the windshield frame (piece 5), then install the motor hood and windshield.

Interior details and paint. I obtained the shape of the floor by tracing along the inside walls of the cab. Don't forget to leave room in the floor for the rear fenders (Fig. 3).

I added just a dash of matte white to the interior of the model, giving it a "dirty" white tint, and painted the steering wheel and gear lever satin black. The dashboard is matte black, the instrument faces highlighted with dry-brushed gloss finish. I weathered the pedals (matte black) heavily, using Rub 'n Buff silver leaf for the look of bare metal. For further weathering, I applied the usual stains: dry mud on the floor (I used Humbrol dark earth, HB2, dry-brushed); scratches of bare metal (same as before, using Rub 'n Buff silver leaf); and oil stains (burnt sienna plus a thin wash of silver).

Exterior. Back to the template: Cut the doors (pieces 6–11). As you can see on the template, the windows on doors 8–11 are slightly off-center: The distance from the vertical edge of the window to the edge of the door is 2 mm on one side, 3 mm on the other. The hinges (made of stretched sprue) are fastened to the narrow edge. The horizontal band that goes around the periphery of the body (Fig. 4) is a 1 mm-wide strip of .010" styrene.

Now add the exterior details: door handles (stretched sprue), turn signals, side-view mirror, access handles to the luggage carrier (stretched sprue), license plates (pieces 17 and 18), and a searchlight on the right side of the vehicle (mine is from the Italeri Opel Blitz, kit No. 216). You'll have to drill new holes for the headlights.

Attach the rear fenders. Cut the rear fender supports (pieces 15 and 16), scribing them along the dotted line so they can be bent (Fig. 6). Add more detail with stretched sprue windshield wipers and width indicators (Fig. 4), which help the truck driver negotiate tight spaces.

Roof. The roof (piece 1) is easy to make. After cutting the piece out of styrene, I glued three layers of .020" styrene, cut to fit just inside the borders of piece 1 (Fig. 5). Then I smoothed the laminated edges with an emery board, repaired rough spots with epoxy putty, and finished the edges with fine-grade sandpaper.

When the roof is complete, make a luggage rack from stretched sprue, then glue it to the roof.

Wheels and windows. After mounting the wheels, I turned my attention to the spare tires that are mounted at the rear of the body on either side. I drilled a hole in the middle of the tire and glued the attaching handles (made from stretched sprue) in place. I added a valve (more stretched sprue!) to each wheel. To make the white shades on my model's windows, I masked the upper fourth of each clear plastic window, then airbrushed them matte white.

Painting. I finished the Granit with a coat of HM4 (Humbrol German Panzer gray). Then I applied an overcoat of Humbrol sea gray medium (HB6). I fixed the base color with a coat of flat finish (diluted 50 percent). Then came what is always the most wearisome part of the process for me—waiting until the next day, when the model would be really dry.

The next day I used a very thin, matte-black wash around details—hinges, handles, air intakes, etc.—immediately dabbing the excess away with a soft rag. This slight tint provides a realistic effect in shadow areas.

I waited five hours before dry-brushing. The first coat was HM4

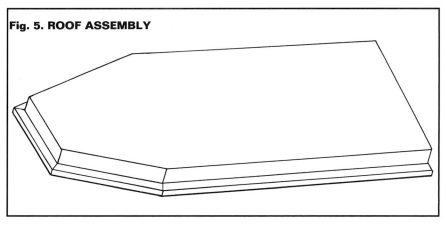

Fig. 5. ROOF ASSEMBLY

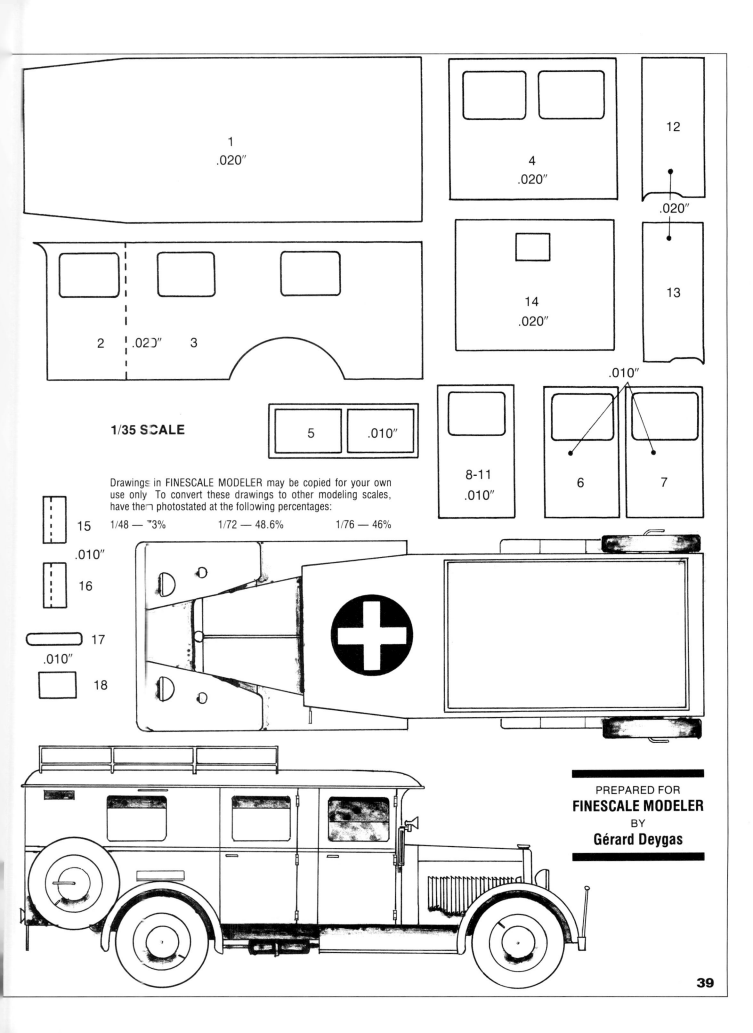

1
.020"

4
.020"

12

.020"

14
.020"

13

2 .020" 3

.010"

1/35 SCALE

5   .010"

8-11
.010"

6   7

1/48 — 73%   1/72 — 48.6%   1/76 — 46%

15

.010"

16

17
.010"

18

PREPARED FOR
FINESCALE MODELER
BY
Gérard Deygas

Fender
support

Fig. 6. The appearance of the unpainted model emphasizes the importance of a good finish. The rear fender supports are styrene, scribed and bent.

I painted the inside of the headlights and searchlight silver, adding a little gloss finish to the latter. The taillight is matte red, also coated with gloss. The license plates are matte white.

I made separate paper patterns for the circle and cross on the roof, painting the circle matte white and the cross matte red. The decals on the doors and the tactical marking on the ambulance's mud flap are from my scrap box.

For a finishing touch, I scraped an ocher pastel pencil (available at artist supply stores) on sandpaper, and gathered the ocher powder with a paintbrush. I applied this powder on the whole lower part of the chassis. Then I blew the surplus of powder from the model. The effect of earth and dust is successfully realistic.

(Panzer gray) with a little HB2 (dark earth). The second coat was an equal mix of HM4 and HB2. Then I finished the dry-brushing with just a hint of matte white.

The windshield wipers are matte black, highlighted with HM4 and HB2. To replicate a rusty exhaust pipe, I painted it with a wash of burnt sienna, waited for that to dry, then dry-brushed a coat of leather matte.

THE PHÄNOMEN GRANIT 1500

The Phänomen Werke Gustav Hiller AG of Zittau, Germany, produced the Granit 1½-ton trucks (models 1500S and 1500A), powered by a 4-cylinder, 4.1-liter, 50 hp air-cooled diesel. During World War Two the German army used the 1500S mainly as an ambulance, and also as a radio-communication vehicle. Only a few of the open-bodied 1500A trucks were produced; some had sand tires and special air filters for their air-cooled engines. These were designed for North Africa, but that campaign ended before they entered service.

For an ambulance, the leaf-spring suspension left much to be desired; the front and rear axles were rigid. The front wheels of the 1500A were driven through a normal differential that was offset to the right of the vehicle. The rear differential, which was in the center, was also a standard type. Both models had a 4-speed transmission, but the 1500A had an auxiliary gear box with two ranges, which doubled the total ratios available.

The early version of the ambulance had an open driving compartment, but later models featured an enclosed driver's cab. The Granit carried four stretchers.

SOURCES
• Rub 'n Buff silver leaf: American Art Clay Inc., 4717 W. 16th Street, Indianapolis, IN 46222
• Sheet styrene: Evergreen Scale Models, 12808 N. E. 125th Way, Kirkland, WA 98034
• Epoxy filler putty: Milliput, Rosemont Hobby Shop, P.O. Box 139, Trexler Mall, Trexlertown, PA 18087

REFERENCES
• Culver, Bruce, *Panzer Colors Vol. II*, Squadron/Signal Publications, Carrollton, Texas, 1978
• Milsom, John, *German Military Transports of World War Two*, Hippocrene Books, New York, 1975
• Spielberger, W. J., and Uwe Feist, *Militärfahrzeuge: German Softskinned Vehicles of WW2*, Aero Publishers, Fallbrook, California, 1970

TAMIYA'S PANTHER Ausf A IN 1/35 SCALE
Reworking and detailing improve a basic armor kit

The finished Panther in its "natural" setting. The Zimmerit coating and paint scheme combine to give a distinctive look to German World War Two armor.

BY GÉRARD DEYGAS

In 1941, the German Army looked for a successor to the PzKpfw IV. The new tank was to be armed with a longer 75 mm cannon, sloped armor (based on experience with the T-34), and larger wheels for better mobility. Daimler-Benz presented the VK 3002 (D-B), a copy of the T-34,

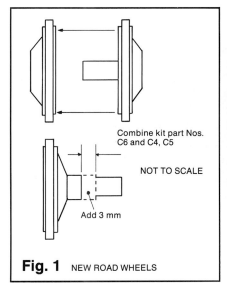

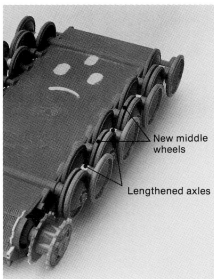

Fig. 1 NEW ROAD WHEELS

Combine kit part Nos. C6 and C4, C5

NOT TO SCALE

Add 3 mm

New middle wheels

Lengthened axles

Fig. 2. The holes from the motorization feature have been filled and the new double wheels and extended axles installed.

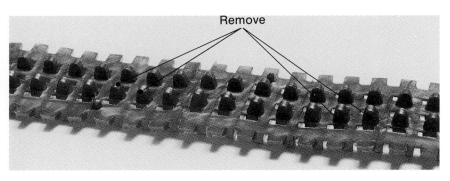

Remove

Fig. 3. Teeth on the tracks must be removed to allow the track to fit on the new wheels. Mark the teeth to be removed when test fitting the track.

and MAN presented the VK 3002 (MAN), which was adopted.

The Panther became available in November 1942, the first real production series being the PzKpfw V Ausf D. During their baptism of fire, in operation Citadelle, they were more susceptible to breakdowns and engine fires than to enemy attacks. The Ausf A version followed and was used at Normandy. Some Panthers were modified to resemble U.S. M10 tank destroyers (see next chapter, "Modeling an Ersatz M10") during the Battle of the Ardennes.

The production objective of 600 vehicles per month was never met because of Allied bombings; maximum output was 330 units. By 1945, 4,800 units were in circulation.

Pressed into service before undergoing proper trials, the Panther initially suffered from mechanical defects. As the problems were resolved the Panther became reliable and respected, and was considered the best German tank of the war.

I started with the Tamiya Panther A kit, reworking and

improving many of the parts. All of the small holding straps, rails, and handles were remade from sheet styrene or stretched sprue. The finished model took a lot of work, but the result is worth it.

Wheels. Each middle road wheel is a double wheel, so eight wheels from a second kit were used to make them accurately. I drilled out the middle with a 6 mm bit and glued them to the single middle wheel. The axle of the outer wheels was extended 3 mm with styrene to allow for the widened middle wheels (Figs. 1 and 2). The road wheels were then put in place and the tracks test fitted. The inside teeth that touched each wheel (two each top and bottom) were marked and cut away to allow the tracks to sit on the modified wheels (Fig. 3).

Three holes were drilled on each side of the chassis over the middle road wheels for rods to help the tracks sit correctly on the wheels. Metal rods were glued in set on a balsa square for support (Fig. 4). I also added a little free pinion wheel from an Italeri kit next to the drive wheel (Fig. 5).

The hull. The first step on the hull consists of filling all the holes in the chassis which were provided for motorization. At the front, I added strengthening plates, each with six nuts, and extended the towing shackles, adding washers and bolt heads (Fig. 5). The tank is coated with Zimmerit, which I engraved using a hot knife with a flat-nose nib. It is a clean, efficient method, but requires practice.

Practice on scrap plastic and regulate the heat intensity until you achieve the desired effect. The underside of the body was blanked off with .020" styrene. To

Fig. 4. The lower hull is shown with two of three metal roads installed to make the tracks sag onto the road wheels.

Fig. 5. The strengthening plates with nuts were made from sheet plastic; the towing shackles were extended to the shape shown and bolt heads added. Also, a new pinion wheel was taken from an Italeri kit.

make the supports for the side armor straps I cut 14 pieces of .010" styrene 5 mm x 3 mm, then folded up 1 mm on each edge. Seven pieces were glued under each side along with a half cylinder at each end (Fig. 6).

I covered the air filters with a piece of wedding veil to simulate the grating; the frames are .010" sheet styrene. The circular cooling vent frames and the handles were replaced with stretched plastic. The small supports on the auxiliary track racks and the tool brackets were cut off and remade from .010" styrene (Fig. 7) along with holding straps of the exhausts. The buckles are made from stretched plastic or fine copper wire.

Turret. The thickness of the periscope was reduced and the edges rounded. All the handles and hooks were remade from stretched sprue. The hook at the head of the cupola is .010" styrene. Because the Tamiya travel lock is inaccurate, I built a replacement from spare parts and styrene. I also replaced the oversized light with one from an Italeri Panzer IV, adding a strip of .010" styrene (Fig. 8).

Side armor. Support straps for the side armor were made by flattening 1 mm copper wire into a strip; I made the front ten from this and the rear four from .020" styrene (Fig. 9). The side armor plates were cut from .020" sheet styrene. I used 6 plates; 12 would make a

full set (Fig. 10). I put a small amount of plastic glue on the straps and placed the plates up to them, allowing the plates to be moved around until their proper position was determined. The plates were then pulled away with their straps attached and the joint strengthened with super glue. I used .010" styrene for the hooks on straps without plates.

The crew is from different kits, the busts coming from Italeri Tank Troops, modified to the poses I wanted.

Painting the Panther. After 1943, German vehicles were painted a base coat of dark sand. The camouflage was olive green and red brown, applied with no

Fig. 6. Here the underside of the body has been blanked off with sheet plastic; seven supports for the side armor are in place.

Fig. 7. All the white pieces are new parts made from plastic. The Zimmerit is engraved into the kit plastic with a hot knife. Note the wedding-veil grating over the air filters.

Fig. 8. The handles and hooks on the turret were added along with a scratchbuilt travel lock. The oversized light was also replaced.

Fig. 9. The mounting straps for the side armor have been loosely placed in the supports prior to fitting the plates.

definite scheme. The paint came in cans of concentrate which was to be diluted with water or gasoline and applied with a spray gun. The tints were unstable and faded when mixed with water, but gasoline was generally too valuable to use. Sometimes the paint was brushed on undiluted.

I mixed Humbrol paints for my colors. After the base colors

dried, I went over all the engraved areas with a diluted black wash. The tracks were painted flat leather No. 62, then silver Rub 'n Buff was brushed on to emphasize worn areas. My rust color is a mix of leather and white, which I added around the grilles, exhausts, and spare track links. The rubber tires on the wheels are a mix of black and gray.

I made two cables from string; stray fibers were eliminated by passing the string through a flame. These were painted leather, then brushed with the powder from a black pastel pencil rubbed on sandpaper. Finally, I added a bucket hanging from the exhaust, an old rag and a helmet in the rear bin, and two thin wires on the glacis plate.

REFERENCES
• Auberbach, William, *Last of the Panzers, German Tanks 1944–45,* Arms and Armour Press, London, 1984
• Culver, Bruce, *Panther in Action,* Squadron/Signal Publications, Carrollton, Texas, 1975
• Lefevre, Eric, *Normandie 1944, Les Panzers,* Heimdal, Bayeux, France, 1978
• Spielberger, Walter J. & Uwe Feist, *The Panther,* Aero Publishers Inc., Fallbrook, California, 1977

Fig. 10. SIDE ARMOR PLATES

1/35 scale template (make 6)

The side armor placed in position; the plates will be pulled off and the straps reinforced with super glue.

AN ERSATZ M10

A simple—and different—armor conversion

Identification quiz: a quick look—M10 tank destroyer, right? Look again. Check out the road wheels. Art's conversion of the little-known German ruse was made from a Nichimo Panther Ausf G. All photos, Brian Gibbs.

BY ART LODER

A well-known part of the legend surrounding the Battle of the Bulge involves English-speaking German troops who used American uniforms and jeeps to get behind Allied lines and cause havoc. Less well known are the similar operations of two companies, Kampfgruppen X and Y of Panzer Brigade 150, which were equipped with heavy vehicles and weapons.

German mastermind Otto Skorzeny had attempted to obtain a number of captured American Sherman tanks, White half-tracks, and M8 scout cars. When few were forthcoming he settled for a number of Sturmgeschütz III assault guns and PzKpfw V Panther Ausf G battle tanks. The Panthers

were altered to resemble American M10 tank destroyers, and were intended to form a unit which was to remain behind the German spearhead until within striking distance of the bridges on the River Meuse. The formation would then be sent forward, pretending to be a retreating American armored column, to seize and hold the bridge until the arrival of the main German force.

The plan might have succeeded had the German advance reached the intended jumping-off point for the disguised unit. But when that objective wasn't met the plan had to be scrapped and the formation was frittered away in conventional engagements. In one of these, American Private Francis Currey won the Medal of

Honor by attacking an ersatz M10 with small arms, forcing its crew to abandon the vehicle.

Wolf in sheep's clothing. The ersatz M10 was basically a PzKpfw V Panther Ausf G with alterations to provide the visual impression (from a distance) of an American M10 tank destroyer.

A new glacis plate was built 7" to 8" in front of the true glacis to cover the characteristic Panther machine gun fitting. The machine gun could be fired through a simple (possibly hinged) cover in the plate. False lift hooks and small fittings were also attached. On the lower bow plate, false differential covers were built and two hooks and a step added. All tool fittings were removed from the sides and the spare track racks were moved

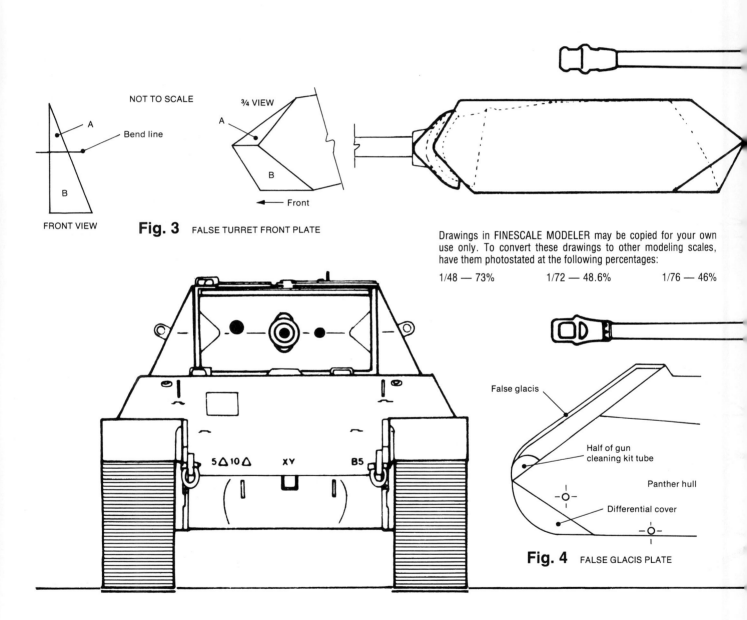

NOT TO SCALE

A

Bend line

B

FRONT VIEW

Fig. 3   FALSE TURRET FRONT PLATE

¾ VIEW

A

B

Front

Drawings in FINESCALE MODELER may be copied for your own use only. To convert these drawings to other modeling scales, have them photostated at the following percentages:

1/48 — 73%   1/72 — 48.6%   1/76 — 46%

5△ 10△   X Y   B5

False glacis

Half of gun cleaning kit tube

Panther hull

Differential cover

Fig. 4   FALSE GLACIS PLATE

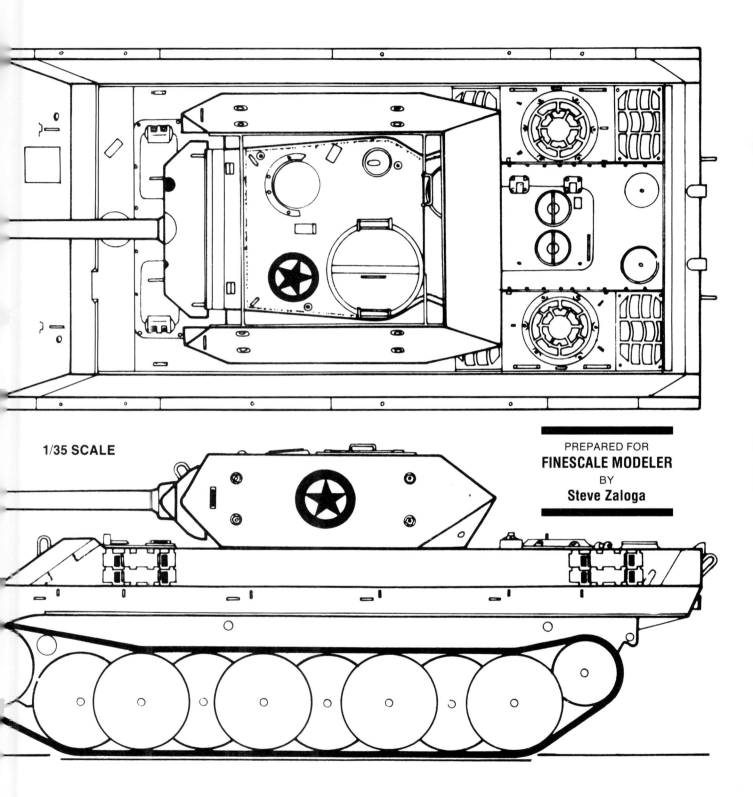

1/35 SCALE

PREPARED FOR
FINESCALE MODELER
BY
Steve Zaloga

Fig. 1. The modifications the Germans made to the Panther were done with sheet metal, so sheet styrene is ideal for modifying the model.

Labels on Fig. 1: Flush turret hatch · False turret side plate · False mantlet · False glacis plate · False side plates · False differential covers

Fig. 2. The false turret sides were attached at the widest point of the Panther turret and the ends were held apart by styrene strips. Note the flush turret hatch, open back end for easy escape, and styrene strip reinforcements.

to locations suitable to an M10. Simple side skirts were also added.

A false rear deck was added to change the characteristic rear overhang of the Panther, requiring the removal of the stowage boxes on the rear corners. Although photographs showing this area are poor, lights and other fittings were probably added. The commander's cupola on the turret was removed entirely and a simple split hatch was substituted. New false turret sides were built, pointed at the front and rear and high enough to camouflage the fact that the turret had a roof, which of course the M10 did not.

At the front a new false mantlet was constructed over the original, with openings for the coaxial machine gun and main sight. The rear of the turret was enclosed at the bottom of the false sides, but photos show no plate fitted at the top, possibly to aid escape from the emergency hatch. Details such as the M10's characteristic turret bolts and lift hooks were added.

The vehicles were painted a dark olive green, and marked as tanks of the American 10th battalion, 5th Armored Division. Known individual numbers are B-4, B-5, B-7, and B-10. American style stars and star-in-circle insignia were applied (not in the same fashion on all vehicles) and Day-Glo orange air identification panels, as used by U.S. armored forces, were carried on the rear deck. In addition, the letters "XY" were added to the bow markings and a yellow triangle was painted on the rear. These were to identify the tank to friendly (German) forces.

Sheet plastic for sheet metal. My ersatz M10 is built from a 1/35 scale Nichimo Panther Ausf G (kit No. N3505) and, although the final model doesn't look a lot like a Panther (or an M10 either, for that matter), it's easy to build. Nearly everything can be accomplished with sheet plastic, Fig. 1.

Since so much of the 1944 prototype consisted of sheet metal panels spot welded over the basic vehicle structure, much of the model can be constructed the same way. I enlarged a Steve Zaloga drawing to 1/35 scale and used it to produce rough templates for the sheet styrene modifications. Starting with the turret, I made side panels from paper, cut them till they were the right shape, transferred them to .015" sheet styrene with a soft pencil, and cut the plastic.

On the real thing, the false turret sides were welded to the widest portion of the turret and were spaced away from the forward and aft ends with rods so they were parallel to the hull sides. I cemented a piece of .015"-square styrene vertically on the turret sides at the widest point to increase the bonding area for the false sides. I also placed two strips forward, one on the turret top and one below the mantlet to hold the sides in position, Fig. 2.

Before I cemented the false sides to the turret, I made .015" triangular plates that fill the gaps adjacent to the mantlet. Through trial and error, I made each of these with one piece of styrene by bending them in the middle. The inner edge must be vertical and the width at the bottom depends on the angle of the side plate, Fig. 3. I cemented the front

Fig. 5. The new front glacis plate features a cutout for the machine gun.

Fig. 6. A trapezoid-shaped piece of sheet styrene was used for the false rear plate.

plates to the false side plates and cleaned up the joints with putty and sandpaper.

Next, I cemented the false side plates to the turret and made new rear panels. I determined the shape of the lower rear panels by measuring with a drafting compass and transferring the measurement to paper. The bottom rear point of the triangle must touch the bottom of the Panther's outer rear plate. Once these plates are attached it's simple to measure the trapezoid-shaped rear plate and fit it. Photos show the real plates were reinforced with welded strips, so I made these from styrene strip.

Glacis plate. The Germans spaced a false glacis plate far enough from the real one to cover the hull machine gun mount. I made an .015" duplicate glacis plate based on the kit hull and positioned it with parallelogram-shaped spacers

at the sides and a half-cylindrical spacer at the bottom made from the gun-cleaning kit tube from the Panther kit, Fig. 4. The space at the top between the false and true glacis plate was filled by a strip of styrene, and a square piece of sheet styrene serves as the machine gun cover. In fitting the false glacis plate, I had to cut out several small areas to clear the tow hooks and fender stiffeners, Fig. 5.

Rear deck. Although there are no good photos of the rear deck area, several assumptions can be made. The new rear plate must be vertical, or nearly so, because to slope it as on the real M10 would produce an extreme overhang. I made the deck extension by fashioning the two side plates first, tacking them to the hull with white glue. I made the trapezoidal lower rear plate by measuring the distances between the ends of the side plates

at top and bottom, Fig. 6. I cemented it between the side plates and attached a top piece to fill in the space between the Panther's deck and the new false plate. I drilled two holes in the new plate for the exhaust pipes and removed the subassembly from the hull by dissolving the white glue with water. Next, I cleaned up the seams and reinstalled the false rear deck with liquid cement.

Mantlet. I built the false mantlet unit the same way as the rear deck; I made the end pieces first and white glued them to the ends of the kit mantlet. I used the compass to measure the upper and lower plates, cut them from .015" styrene, and cemented them to the end pieces (not to the kit mantlet). The remaining triangular pieces were fitted by the cut-and-try method. After the false mantlet assembly was set, I

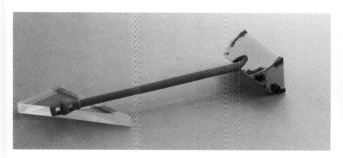

Fig. 7. The new mantlet was fashioned from .015" styrene.

Fig. 8. Art found the false differential covers to be the most difficult parts to make.

49

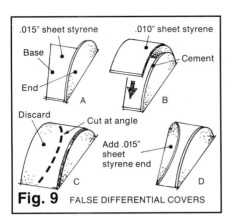

Fig. 9 FALSE DIFFERENTIAL COVERS

.015" sheet styrene
Base
End
A

.010" sheet styrene
Cement
B

Discard
Cut at angle
C

Add .015" sheet styrene end
D

Fig. 10. Sheet styrene was again used for the false hull side plates.

dissolved the white glue, removed it from the model, and reinforced the insides of the joints with super glue. The joints were cleaned up, puttied, and sanded smooth, Fig. 7.

Differential covers. I cut a trapezoid-shaped piece of .015" plastic for the back to fit against the hull lower front plate, Fig. 8. The outside end (nearest the track) piece was made by tracing the arc of the lower front side plate of the Panther onto .015" sheet plastic, Fig. 9. I cemented it at a 90-degree angle to the backing piece.

Next, I attached a piece of .010" styrene from one edge of the base piece to the other, gently bending the plastic over the arc as I bonded it with super glue. When this was set, I cut away the excess

plastic to form the inner edge.

The last piece is the inner face made from an .015" sheet super glued to the open end. A mate for the other side was fashioned in the same way, all seams sanded smooth, and both differential covers were cemented to the lower front plate.

Details and finish. The side skirts were cut from sheet styrene, Fig. 10, while the new turret split hatch was made with a circle cutter from two discs of .010" styrene and detailed with Grandt Line hinges and bent plastic rod handles. I also used Grandt Line nut/bolt/washer castings on the turret sides. I scrounged hooks and lift rings from scrap and my spare parts box—the taillights came from an Italeri Leopard A4 kit. The spare track sections from the Panther kit were cut into three sections and mounted on the hull sides.

I whipped up a shade of olive drab designed to look slightly different from the U. S. standard. I left the inner hull under the fenders, behind the wheels, and the back sides of the wheels German Armor Dark Sand, but these areas aren't easily seen, so you can paint them olive drab, too.

The lettering and stars came from Microscale U.S. armor decal sheet No. 13-0008. My model represents a vehicle with the turret and bow stars in circles. It appears the Germans applied these insignias over a blue background—remember, they didn't have official U.S. Army marking specifications handy! I applied white bow codes, reading 5A10A XY B10, and a yellow triangle on the rear plate. I made the Day-Glo orange air-identification panel on the rear deck from tissue, Fig. 11.

Weathering should be light, as these vehicles were built specifically for the Ardennes offensive. The markings on the vehicles varied, but the Pallud book listed shows all four known ersatz M10s.

REFERENCES
• Gibbs, Brian, Art Loder, and Stephen Zaloga, "Operation Griffon-Panzer Brigade 150," *IPMS Quarterly*, Vol. 10, No. 2, 1975
• Pallud, Jean Paul, *The Battle of the Bulge—Then and Now*, After the Battle, London, 1984
• Spielberger, Walter, *Der Panzerkampfwagen Panther und seine Abarten*, 1978

SOURCES
• Plastic bolt heads, hinges, and stirrup step: Grandt Line Products, Inc., 1040B Shary Court, Concord, CA 94518
• Sheet and strip styrene: Evergreen Scale Models, 12808 N. E. 125th Way, Kirkland, WA 98034

Fig. 11. The yellow triangle on the rear plate was an identification mark to alert German troops that this was not really an American vehicle. Note the orange air-identification panel on the rear deck.

BUILDING A MARINE CORPS M4A2 IN 1/35 SCALE

Resin conversion kits backdate Tamiya's M4A3 Sherman

Joe converted Tamiya's 1/35 scale Sherman M4A3 to an M4A2, then dressed it up to go wading in the Pacific Ocean. Resin conversion kits helped make the change.

BY JOE P. MORGAN

No collection of World War II armor models would be complete without at least one Sherman. I'm an ex-Marine and the son of a WWII Marine, so naturally I wanted to build a Marine Corps Sherman. I modeled an early production M4A2, distinguished by its 56-degree front-hull slope, protruding driver's hatches, and single turret hatch. (Later M4A2s had a 47-degree slope on the front, flush drivers' hatches, and a loader's hatch on the turret roof.)

I backdated Tamiya's 1/35 scale M4A3 (kit No. 35122) by replacing the upper hull, the lower rear hull panel, and the turret with two Verlinden resin conversion kits: the early Sherman M34 turret (kit No. 334) and the M4A2 welded hull (No. 333). It would be less expensive to simply modify the Tamiya turret by filling in its M4A3 details, the loader hatch and smoke mortar. However, I avoided restoring the cast-iron finish to the modified areas.

I added Verlinden's photoetched brass Sherman Super Detail set (No. 263) and A. E. F. Designs' Marine Wading Gear (WS-45), as well as other details. Fig. 1 shows the major elements of my conversion.

An indispensable reference for my M4A2 was *Sherman: A History of the American Medium Tank,* by R. P. Hunnicutt, featuring hundreds of photos as well as drawings by D. P. Dyer.

The right track. I didn't want grousers on my tracks, so I used a Top Brass Sherman track kit (kit No. 2-TB3005). However, you can cut the grousers from the Tamiya tracks with a hobby knife

or scissors. Keep the cut edge to the inside, and the modification is barely noticeable.

Cast-resin parts. All the Verlinden and A. E. F. parts (except the photoetched detail set) are resin. Trim and sand resin as you would styrene, but remember that resin is more brittle. Be careful of small raised details: I knocked off one of the rear towing eyes (of course it disappeared in my carpet).

Plastic cement won't work on resin parts; you must use super glue. It sets quickly, so work fast. Always test fit pieces first. Whenever you can, position the parts, touch the applicator tip to the seam, and let capillary action carry glue along the mating surfaces.

Hull preparation. I blocked my electric finishing sander upside down and removed a large lip of flash from the bottom of the

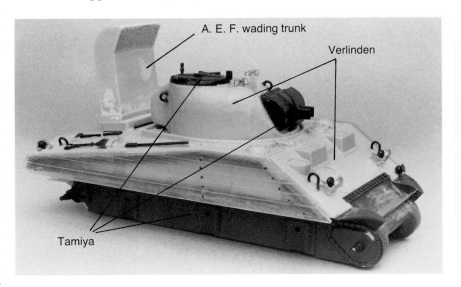

Fig. 1. The dark areas are from the Tamiya kit. Verlinden and A. E. F. resin conversion kits allowed Joe to choose his Sherman variant. And the wood armor? Read on!

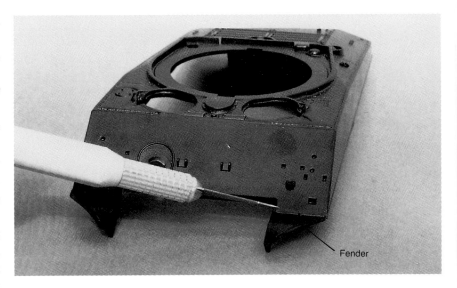

Fig. 2. Cut the fenders from the Tamiya kit and install them on the Verlinden hull. Cut off more than you need, then trim each fender to fit. Joe detailed the fender with brass braces.

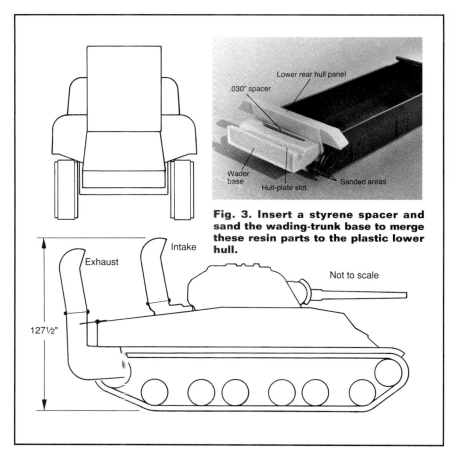

Fig. 3. Insert a styrene spacer and sand the wading-trunk base to merge these resin parts to the plastic lower hull.

Exhaust
Intake
Not to scale
127½"

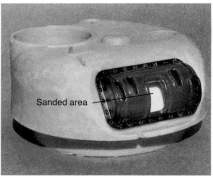

Sanded area

Fig. 4. Joe sawed the Verlinden mantlet as much as he could. Then he got out the elbow grease and started filing and sanding.

Verlinden hull. (You can use a knife, but I prefer to let the machine do the work.) Look at the Tamiya hull to determine how much of the Verlinden hull is flash. Take it easy, and check your progress often. I also cut off the gun travel lock's small brackets.

The Verlinden hull has no front fenders; get them from the Tamiya hull (Fig. 2). Use a knife or a razor saw and cut close to the hull so you get the whole fender, then trim it to fit. Set the fenders aside; they're easier to align after the hull halves are joined.

Rear hull panel and wading gear. To fit the rear wading-trunk base, you must remove the mufflers and exhaust pipes from the Verlinden rear hull panel. I know, I know— the casting is nice, but if you keep the exhaust you have to hollow the bottoms of the wading

trunks (they're cast solid). You wouldn't see the cast detail anyway. I used a razor saw, being careful not to scratch outside the area of the wading trunks. (I still left a few gouges.)

Modify part 1 (the base) of the wading trunk to clear the rear hull (Fig. 3). I cut a ⅛" x ³⁄₁₆" slot to accept the hull plate. To make sure I had enough "meat" to work with, I made a spacer from .030" sheet styrene, traced from the wader base and trimmed to fit. Glue the spacer to the spot formerly occupied by the mufflers. Sand the beveled corners on the wader base to clear the bolt heads on the idler wheel (Fig. 3).

Each piece of the wading gear must be doctored to fit. Don't be discouraged; it took me about three hours to prepare these parts. Once you know how to attach the

wading gear, you're ready to build the tank.

According to the instructions— at first. Follow Tamiya's Step 1 for the suspension, paint these parts, and set them aside.

In Step 2 (the rear panel and wheels), sand parts B9 and B10 to clear the wader base. Glue the rear-panel assembly and the forward lower plate to the lower hull, Step 3 (Fig. 3).

I left off the suspension until after painting. The towing pintle (B11) won't clear the wading gear; leave it off, but attach the pintle bracket (B12).

Mantlet and turret. I skipped ahead to the turret. The Verlinden turret has the earlier M34 mantlet, and my tank needed the M34A1 mantlet supplied in the Tamiya kit. I sawed away as much of the Verlinden mantlet as I could, then filed and sanded it nearly flush (Fig. 4).

The Tamiya mantlet must also be modified (Fig. 5). Cut off the mounts on part C16 (the gun shield). Because the Verlinden turret is solid, there is no room for part C13 (the gun-barrel retainer). Sand the outer edge of C16 (where the screws are) to about half its thickness; refer to

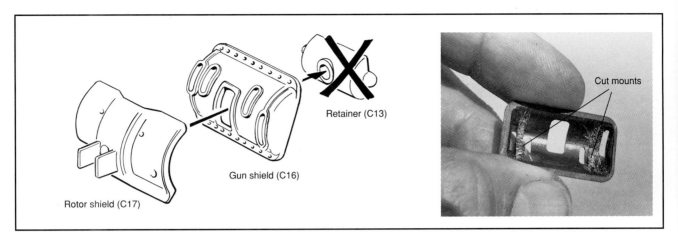

Cut mounts

Retainer (C13)

Gun shield (C16)

Rotor shield (C17)

Fig. 5. MANTLET

Sherman photos. Bevel the inner edges of C16 to fit over what's left of the Verlinden mantlet, then glue C16 to the turret. Glue C17 (the rotor shield) directly to C16. The elevation of the gun will be fixed, so choose now.

Add the Verlinden periscope and the Tamiya parts per the instructions, but leave off parts C1, C14, B16, and the .50 caliber machine gun. Use the Tamiya hatch, parts C2, C3, and C11. The antenna is stretched sprue.

I super glued Verlinden pho-toetched periscope guards (Fig. 6) using a needle-nose forceps to bend and form these parts. Glue two of the four legs. After they dry, it's easy to fit the other legs.

Upper hull. You don't have to stow all the tools; they often vanished, to the eternal dismay of supply officers. But if you leave off a tool, keep its attachment fitting. I secured tools with "cable" made of nylon cord stiffened with gun-metal paint (Fig. 7). You'll have to alter some of the Tamiya tools to stow them on the Verlinden hull.

I replaced the Tamiya headlight and taillight guards with photoetched parts shaped around a paintbrush handle and bent to fit (Fig. 6). I used the same trick I had with the periscope guards, gluing one side of the part, adjusting, then gluing the rest of the part.

Now install the forward (intake) wading trunk (Fig. 6). Sand off the rear engine-grille hinges so the trunk will sit flat on the deck. I used masking tape to replicate the waterproof tape that seals the trunk sections (Fig. 7).

Join the upper and lower hull, then install the fenders you set aside earlier. Fit the fenders one at a time: They require lots of sanding, shaving, and grumbling. The fenders were too wide for the Verlinden hull, so I built up the inside edge of the hull mounting surface with styrene. I made sheet-metal fender braces from the brass parts runner (Fig. 8).

Spare tracks are stowed on the front glacis plate, so omit the Tamiya racks (A12 and A13). Single track blocks were spot-welded to the hull, so I simply glued them. However, the large horizontal section of track on the front requires a mount; I made one from 3 mm Plastruct angle, shaved

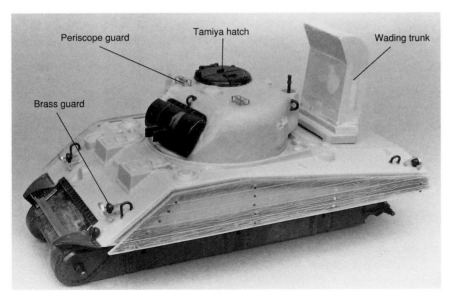

Periscope guard

Tamiya hatch

Wading trunk

Brass guard

Fig. 6. Photoetched details, such as the light and periscope guards, are a fancy touch. You don't have to stow all the tools, but be sure to include their retaining brackets.

Fig. 7. Joe replicated towing cable with nylon cord that he dipped in gunmetal paint. He "waterproofed" the waders with masking tape.

Fig. 8. Details make the difference: Here's what's up front.

to scale (Fig. 8). It held the track and provided a mount for the upright fender braces. I cut the Tamiya tracks, parts B51, and rejoined them to make one section that fit (exactly!) between the fenders.

Extra armor. Tank crews inspired by the survival instinct devised many ingenious ways to add armor to their vehicles. Spare tank treads and other bulky chunks of metal were stowed strategically on the hull. Sherman crews sometimes bolted lumber to the hull and poured concrete in

the gap between the lumber and the tank.

I modeled my extra "armor" after a photo on page 20 of Steven J. Zaloga's *Armour of the Pacific War* of a Sherman with 2" x 6" planks fitted to the sides. I scribed "planks" in .060" sheet styrene (about 2 scale inches thick). Scribing is easier than cutting and texturing individual planks. I mounted the wood armor on 3 mm Plastruct angle (Fig. 9).

Make two copies of the template in Fig. 10 and use clear tape

to attach each template to .060" styrene sheet. Before cutting the sheet with a fine-tooth saber saw, I covered the sheet with masking tape to protect it from the saw and to ease marking and scribing. Scribe the planks with a utility knife. (Don't worry about slight irregularities; the real planks were rough cuts.) Scribe the wood grain in the plastic with the edge of a hobby knife. About ⅛" of the inside face will show, so scribe planks and grain there, too. Cut lines in the sheet edges to

Fig. 9. Joe made the wood-armor mount from Plastruct angle, roughing up the outside edges to replicate concrete.

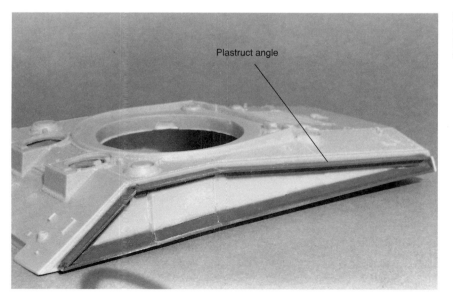

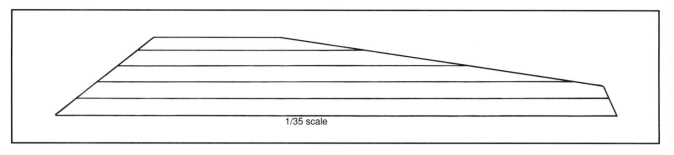

1/35 scale

Fig. 10 TEMPLATE

match the scribed planks (Fig. 11).

I gouged the Plastruct edges to replicate the concrete poured between the planks and the hull, then filled remaining gaps with .030" strip. I cinched the attachment bolts with lug nuts from my spares box, but you can use Grandt Line nuts (Fig. 11).

Paint and markings. I blended Tamiya dark green and white and painted most of the model U.S. Marine green. Shermans were delivered in Army olive drab, and I painted some parts this color, reasoning that Marine painters would have skipped inaccessible areas.

My old Mark 83 radio jeep was the color reference. Originally Marine green, it had faded under the sun of Southern California and Hawaii.

I dry-brushed a lighter green, then added olive drab, gunmetal, and a little reddish brown in high-wear areas where the top coat of paint might be scuffed or worn through to the bare metal. A dark wash around the engine deck replicates fuel and oil spills.

The machine guns are black, dry-brushed with gunmetal. The main gun is green, except for light gray at the mantlet and black discoloration at the muzzle. I painted

the engine and the wading-trunk grilles black for an illusion of depth, then dry-brushed green to highlight details. The headlight bulbs are painted white, with an "eyebrow" of gunmetal. I painted the camouflage net dark green, spotted it brown, and dry-brushed it a lighter green.

The upper rear hull is white, a conclusion I drew from black-and-white photos. (I suppose this air-recognition mark could have been gray.)

Next I installed the remaining wading gear. The exhaust-trunk braces, detailed with lug nuts, are from my parts box (Fig. 7).

I designated my tank "Joker" of C Company, 4th Tank Battalion, in action on Namur in the

Marshall Islands. The battalion markings are Woodland Scenics dry transfers.

Still searching. I was frustrated by the scarcity of information on Shermans in U.S. Marine service. It was even difficult to find an exact number of Sherman M4A2s delivered to the United States Marine Corps. My estimate is 500, based on figures provided by Hunnicutt in *Sherman*. Special thanks go to John G. Griffith of the U.S. Marine Corps museum at Quantico, Virginia, for his assistance.

Not counting research, I spent more than 40 hours building "Joker." Without the wading gear this would have been an easy conversion—but not as interesting!

Fig. 11. You can detail a field-fit with almost any size hardware. Joe recommends Grandt Line nuts.

Nut

Planks

SEAGOING SHERMANS

In the amphibious assaults of World War II, unarmed landing craft delivering tanks were easy targets for shore gunners.

During preparations for D-day, British Maj. Gen. Percy C. Hobart introduced several innovations for amphibious operations. Among them was the Sherman DD (Duplex Drive). A rubberized canvas screen attached to the tank hull and raised on steel arms, displaced enough water to keep the tank afloat. Twin propellers hung from hinges on the rear of the tank.

Despite the theory that tanks discharged offshore would have a better chance at survival, Americans were skeptical of these British "Funnies." In fact, many DDs sank in the rough seas off Normandy on June 6, 1944. But the ones that made it ashore provided valuable support for Allied troops.

In the Pacific Shermans were fitted with deep-water fording kits. Sheet metal covers and tall exhaust and intake ducts ("trunks") were sealed with waterproof tape. Metal straps held the exhaust duct in place; bolts secured the intake. With additional waterproofing, these tanks operated in surf as deep as six feet. Because the wading trunks limited turret movement, they were removed immediately upon landing.

SOURCES
• Sherman Marine wading gear: A. E. F. Designs, 14413 E. 47th Ave., Denver, CO 80239
• Scale nuts and bolts: Grandt Line Products, 1040B Shary Court, Concord, CA 94518
• Styrene sheet, strip, and angle: Plastruct, 1020 S. Wallace Place, City of Industry, CA 91748
• Top Brass Sherman track kit: available from Squadron Shop, 1115 Crowley Drive, Carrollton, TX 75011-5010
• Resin Sherman M4A2 hull, resin Sherman M34 turret: Verlinden Productions, Lone Star Industrial Park, 811 Lone Star Drive, O'Fallon, MO 63366
• Dry-transfer lettering: Woodland Scenics, P.O. Box 98, Linn Creek, MO 65052

REFERENCES
• Forty, George, *M4 Sherman*, Blandford Press, London, 1987
• Hunnicutt, R. P., Sherman: *A History of the American Medium Tank*, Presidio Press, Novato, California, 1978
• Zaloga, Steven J., *Armour of the Pacific War*, Osprey Publishing, London, 1983

BUILDING A PANZERWERFER 42 IN 1/35 SCALE

Adding armor and rockets to Testor/Italeri's Opel Maultier

A scratchbuilt 15 cm Nebelwerfer and sheet-styrene armor convert an Opel Maultier to a Panzerwerfer 42.

BY DAN TISONCIK

The Panzerwerfer 42 was a lightly armored Opel Maultier halftrack developed by Germany in World War II as a mobile mount for the Nebelwerfer, or rocket launcher. Nebelwerfers were lighter and more versatile than field artillery.

Ten 15 cm barrels, arranged in two tiers, delivered smoke screens and massed fire. However, the smoke trail drew enemy fire and limited the time a launcher could stay in action before withdrawing.

The Panzerwerfer 42 could move to cover for reloading. Its 7/32" armor protected the crew from small arms fire. A 7.92 mm MG34 pintle-mounted machine gun sat on the cab. The Nebelwerfer traversed 360 degrees and elevated 80 degrees.

My model is based on Testor/ Italeri's 1/35 scale Opel Maultier, kit No. 0221. I used the kit-supplied chassis, running gear, and motor, and scratchbuilt the rest from sheet plastic, putty, lead foil, and aluminum tubing, Fig. 1.

Lower body. I used McKean 2 mm styrene tread plate, Fig. 2. (If you don't model an interior, regular sheet styrene will do.) Cut it slightly oversized and trim it according to the template in Fig. 3. Install the lower side plates, angling them outward from the floor, Fig. 4; bevel the mating edges for a better fit. Interior bulkheads support the plates. You can add styrene blocks and strips for further reinforcement. Since I was going to leave the rear open, I moved the engine fire wall to the front, Fig. 5.

Upper body. Using the templates (Fig. 6), I cut .5 mm sheet styrene for front, back, and upper body plates. Set the front and rear plates aside. Glue the side plates,

Fig. 1. The elements of Dan's conversion: a scratchbuilt body and a kit-supplied chassis.

Fig. 2. The floor is tread-patterned sheet styrene. If you don't want to build a fancy interior, keep the door closed.

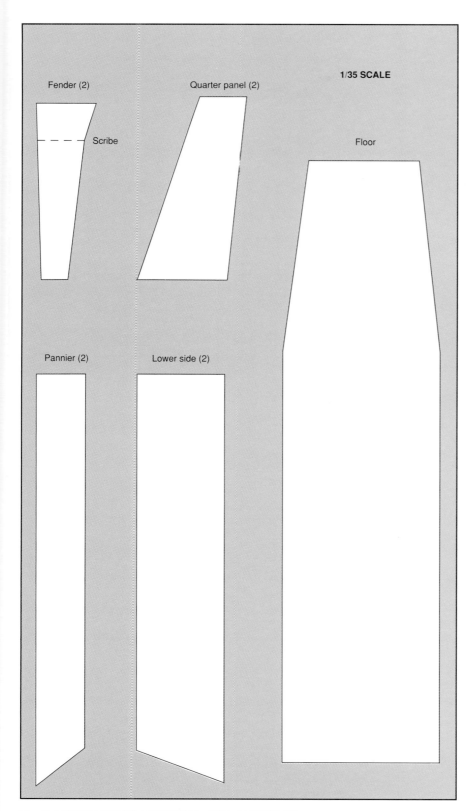

Fig. 3. LOWER BODY, FENDERS, AND STOWAGE

Within the diagram:

Fender (2)

Scribe

Quarter panel (2)

1/35 SCALE

Floor

Pannier (2)

Lower side (2)

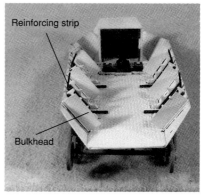

Reinforcing strip

Bulkhead

Fig. 4. The sides angle out from the floor. Styrene bulkheads and strips reinforce their structure.

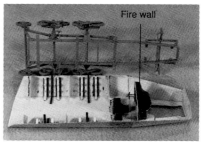

Fire wall

Fig. 5. Dan moved the fire wall forward in his interior scheme.

driver's compartment with a firewall, dashboard, steering wheel, seats, vision blocks, radio, instruments, field equipment, and weapons. I detailed the rear with 12 scratchbuilt ammo racks carved from 1/4" styrene blocks and mounted to the walls with Plastruct channel and Grandt Line bolts, Fig. 9. The lock-down bars are strip styrene and stretched sprue. Paint the interior Testor's camouflage white flat, then weather with black washes and drybrushing.

Making the body whole. Now it's time put the body together, Fig. 10—and easier said than done. You'll need lots of putty and patience. Close off the cab by adding the front grille, a hexagonal piece of styrene with a cutout in which I mounted five movable

angling them out from the roof, Fig. 7. Putty and file the edges for a smooth fit along the joints.

Interior details. Before fitting the body to the chassis I built an interior, Fig. 8. I dressed up the

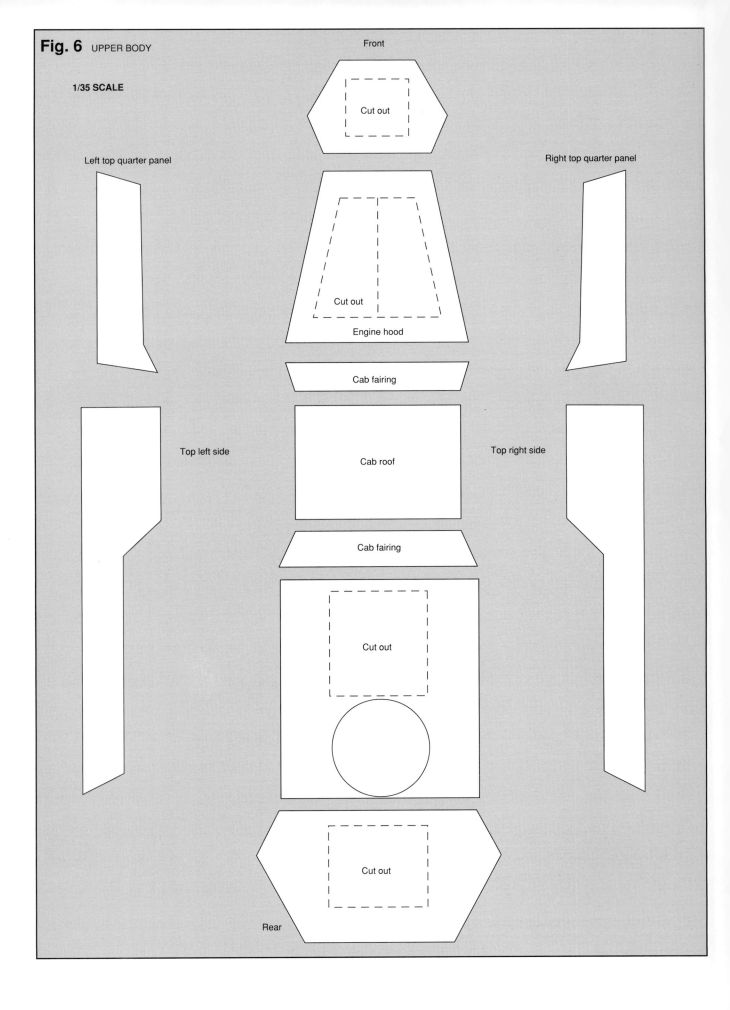

Fig. 6 UPPER BODY

1/35 SCALE

Front

Cut out

Left top quarter panel

Right top quarter panel

Cut out

Cut out

Engine hood

Cab fairing

Top left side

Cab roof

Top right side

Cab fairing

Cut out

Cut out

Rear

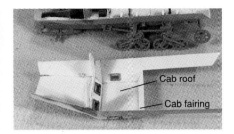

Cab roof

Cab fairing

Engine hood

Fig. 7. The upper plates angle out from the roof. You can simply scribe the engine hood, or you can open it up.

slats that can be posed open or closed, Fig. 11. In front of the slats are protective bars made of sprue.

A larger hexagonal piece brings up the rear of the vehicle; this plate also has a cutout. I dressed up the doors with hinges and scribed details.

Cut side-stowage panniers and front fenders from .100 mm sheet according to the templates in Fig. 3. I scribed individual compartments in the panniers and added locks and hinges.

Additional details include front and rear towing pintles; jerry-can stowage racks; a rear step; M. V. Products lenses for headlights; air-intake covers; an MG34 and antiaircraft gun mount; wire grab handles; locking

mechanisms on the insides of the doors; and more than 300 rivets, each cut from .010" sheet styrene, carefully positioned on the vehicle, then sanded.

Nebelwerfer. The most difficult part of my model was aligning the rocket tubes, Fig. 12. I cut them from 5/32" aluminum tubing and thinned the ends with a hobby knife.

Carve Nebelwerfer mounts from 1/2" block styrene. Cut tube supports from .010" sheet according to the template, Fig. 12. To cut holes for each tube, punch the sheet with a compass point, carefully cut out the hole with a hobby knife, then insert the tube. Four supports are needed: Insert, align, and glue the first row of tubes, do

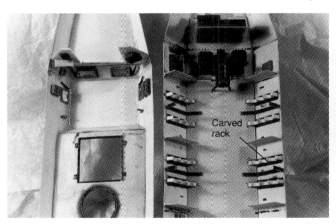

Carved rack

Fig. 8. As details are added the driver's compartment and rear compartment begin to take shape.

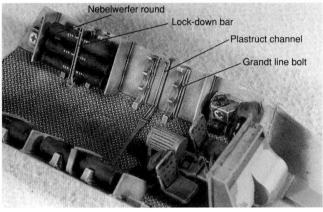

Nebelwerfer round

Lock-down bar

Plastruct channel

Grandt line bolt

Fig. 9. Plastruct structural shapes, styrene sheet, stretched sprue, and Grandt Line bolts provide the hardware.

Fig. 10. You've come this far—don't lose patience now! Fitting the body halves together takes time—and putty.

Movable slats

Fig. 11. The radiator is covered by five movable slats.

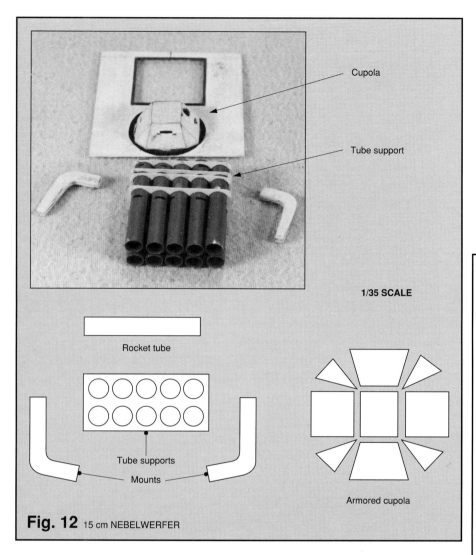

Cupola

Tube support

1/35 SCALE

Rocket tube

Tube supports

Mounts

Armored cupola

Fig. 12 15 cm NEBELWERFER

detailed with handles and Verlinden dry-transfer lettering.

Painting. I applied a base coat of Humbrol Panzer yellow and followed with a thin wash of burnt-sienna oil. Then I dry-brushed with dark earth and lighter shades of the base color. To depict charring rocket exhaust, blacken the ends of the tubes with powdered pastel chalk.

SOURCES
• Pastel chalks: Duro Art Industries, 1832 Juneway, Chicago, IL 60626
• Bolt heads: Grandt Line Products, Inc., 1040B Shary Court, Concord, CA 94518
Epoxy putty:
• A+B Putty, Biggs Co., 612 E. Franklin, El Segundo, CA 90245
• Milliput, Rosemont Hobby Shop, P.O. Box 139, Trexler Mall, Trexlertown PA 18087
• Headlight lenses: M. V. Products, Inc., P.O. Box 6622, Orange, CA 92667
Metal tubing:
• Brass, K&S Engineering, 6917 W. 59th St., Chicago, IL 60638
• Stainless steel, Small Parts Incorporated, 13980 N. W. 58th Court, Miami Lakes, FL 33138
Styrene rod, tube, sheet, and tread plate:
• Evergreen, 12808 N. E. 128th Way, Kirkland, WA 98034
• McKean, available from Wm. K. Walthers, P.O. Box 18676, Milwaukee, WI 53218
• Plastruct, 1020 S. Wallace Place, City of Industry, CA 91748

REFERENCES
• Hancock, David, "A Make-Do Maultier," *Military Modeling* magazine, Argus Specialist Publications, Hemel Hempstead, Hertsfordshire, England, March 1978
• Meserve, J. "Maultier Panzerwerfer," *Military Modeler* magazine, Challenge Publications, Canoga Park, California, November 1984
• Milson, John, *German Half-Tracks of WWII*, Arms and Armour Press, London, 1975

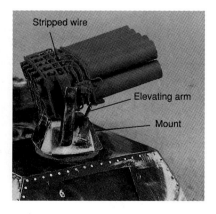

Stripped wire

Elevating arm

Mount

Fig. 13. Super details: Stripped telephone wire, an elevating arm, and Grandt Line bolts finish the Nebelwerfer.

the same for the second, then move on to the next support. I used stripped telephone wire for the weapon wiring and added Grandt Line bolt heads, Fig. 13.

Cupola and ammo. Cut the cupola from .100 mm sheet, Fig. 12, and glue it together. Sand the mounts to shape and install the Nebelwerfer, Fig. 13. I added an elevating arm and ran wires from the junction boxes to the support arms.

I sculpted 10 rocket rounds for the launcher and made stowage for 10 more from aluminum tubing, painted and

MODEL A U.S. M3A1 STUART IN 1/35 SCALE

Converting Tamiya's M3 light tank

It doesn't take an expert to convert Tamiya's M3 to an M3A1. Building a new, welded turret from sheet styrene is more than half the battle.

BY PAUL KRYLOWSKI

The easiest way to model an M3A1 is to convert Tamiya's 1/35 scale M3 Stuart (kit No. 35042).

Rearrange a few details, replicate weld seams, and you're in business —or so I thought. When I compared the kit to scale drawings, I was surprised to find the turret was undersized; the kit's turret-base fairing should be the actual diameter of the turret. What started as an easy modification suddenly became complicated.

Fig. 1. Idler arm details, made from styrene scraps.

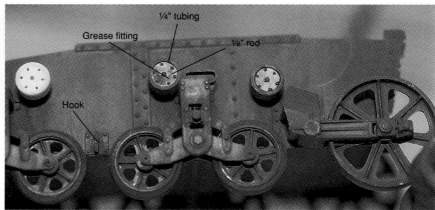

Fig. 2. New return rollers made of styrene tube and rod, detailed with stretched-sprue bolts. The hook is also stretched sprue.

Lower hull. I started the lower hull by painting it with a base coat of Pactra olive drab, weathering it with Tamiya olive drab and a mix of Polly S field drab and earth yellow, and finally dry-brushing with Tamiya olive drab darkened slightly with Tamiya German gray. Because more work would be needed on the front and rear plates after joining the hull halves, I painted those surfaces later.

Suspension. I replaced the idler arm's track tension device, a large nut-and-screw combination, with a new nut made from .030" sheet styrene and stretched sprue to replicate a threaded rod. I also hollowed and reshaped the molded idler arm mount, Fig. 1.

I carved two hooks from .030" sheet styrene and attached them on either side of the hull between the second and third road wheels, Fig. 2. The base plates for these two hooks are molded on the hull.

To make new return rollers, I inserted ⅛" styrene rod in ¼" styrene tubing and added stretched-sprue details: six bolts on each wheel and a grease fitting on the hub, Fig. 2. I painted the rubber on the road wheels, return rollers, and tracks Tamiya dark gray.

Upper hull. Depending on when it was produced, an M3A1 might have a fully riveted hull or a combination of riveted and welded surfaces with a rolled rear overhang. If you model an M3A1 with rivets on the hull side, keep the kit's riveted back plate. If you model the partially welded hull (as I did), remove the rivets and tie-downs.

I reinforced the inside of the back plate with strip-styrene scraps, then shaped it with a file. Although I didn't break through the plastic, the part would have been too weak to withstand the work without reinforcement. Drawing the curve of this plate on masking tape and attaching the tape to the hull gave me a guide for filing.

After protecting rear-deck details with masking tape I cut out the molded intake vent and built a new intake from .020" sheet, Fig. 3. I replaced the screen with Scale Scenics Micro-Mesh aluminum HO scale fencing. (It's easy to cut and shape; ask for it at model railroad hobby shops.)

Fig. 3. Need intake screening? Try HO scale aluminum fencing.

Fig. 4. Bigger turret, bigger turret ring; strip styrene does the trick.

Fuel drums

Fig. 5. Aquarium tubing makes a good fuel drum. The drum lids are .060" styrene disks; details are .015" sheet and stretched sprue.

Turret ring. Carefully slice off the molded details around the ring and set them aside. Make a new ring from .015" strip styrene, Fig. 4. Glue down one end of the strip and wrap it around the turret ring until it overlaps. Cut off the overlap, smooth the ends, and glue them together. Strengthen the joint with liquid cement. Repeat with one or two more strips, staggering the joints to avoid making a bulge, until you build the ring out to the front edge of the top deck. File the top of the new ring flush with the molded ring and reattach the details you removed earlier.

Fuel drums. To extend their range, Stuarts carried external auxiliary fuel drums. The retaining brackets could be activated from inside the tank to jettison them. This mechanism was mounted on a base plate.

I prepared to mount the auxiliary fuel drums by cutting off the armored gas-cap housings. The drums are made from rigid ½" aquarium tubing, available wherever aquarium supplies are sold. I traced the tube ends on .060" sheet styrene, drawing two circles; the outer circle was the diameter of the drum, the inner circle a

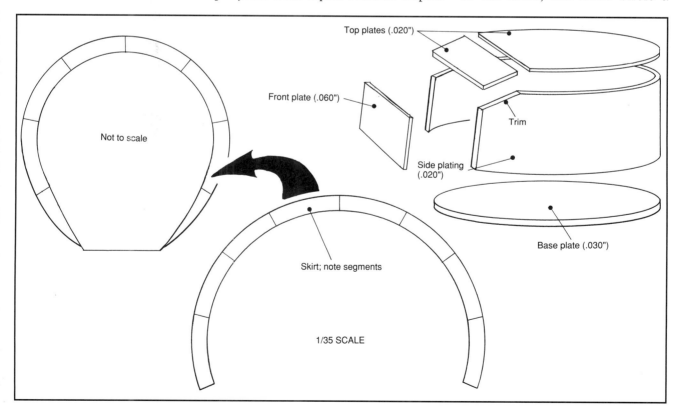

Not to scale

Top plates (.020")

Front plate (.060")

Trim

Side plating (.020")

Base plate (.030")

Skirt; note segments

1/35 SCALE

Fig. 6. TURRET AND SKIRT

Fig. 7. Most of the dark parts are from the kit; the white parts are sheet and strip styrene. Stretched sprue replicates weld beads.

Fig. 8. Nearly ready to roll into action: Styrene add-ons are easy to spot on the unpainted model.

reference for attaching a motor tool. I cut the large circle slightly oversize, super glued it to my motor-tool shank, and chucked it in the motor tool.

Wearing safety glasses, I used my tool as a lathe, shaping the spinning plastic with a chisel-pointed hobby knife. I super glued the finished disks to the tube ends and made the rest of the fuel-drum details from .015" sheet styrene and stretched sprue, Fig. 5.

To use a motor tool as a lathe you must slow it down. You can buy a speed reducer, but I made my own by wiring a receptacle with a dimmer switch. (Warning! Don't try this without proper training in making 110 volt AC connections.)

Turret. Oh sure, you could buy a resin kit of the M3A1 turret, but I scratchbuilt mine from sheet styrene, Fig. 6. I modeled it after a real M5 at a nearby American Legion post; the M5 turret has the same basic shape.

To make a turret base plate, I transferred the top view of the turret from scale drawings to .030" sheet, then moved in .020" to allow for the thickness of the side plating (.020" sheet). I cut an

opening in the base plate for the turret ring.

For the side plating, I bent .020" sheet around the base plate, test fitting to find the needed length of sheet. I glued the side plating around the base plate, taping it in position as I worked my way around.

I made the angled top of the turret from two pieces of .020" sheet, carving the side plating to match the angle at the turret front and smoothing the joints with epoxy putty. The front turret plate, glued to the other plates' outer faces, is .060" sheet styrene.

The toughest part of the turret proved to be the skirt that flares out from the bottom. I attached a hobby-knife blade to the pencil end of a compass, scribed a sheet of .010" styrene, and punched the piece out of the sheet. Figure 6 provides a template for this piece. I cut it in eight sections to attach it to the bottom of the turret, smoothing the joints with putty.

I finished the turret joints with stretched sprue to replicate weld beads, laying in thin beads of sprue and brushing them with liquid cement until they softened.

Then I textured them with a hobby knife.

By moving the turret mounting-ring tabs, I only have to turn the turret a few degrees to drop it into place. Without this modification I wouldn't be able to get my turret past the fuel drums and onto the hull.

I detailed my turret with .030" sheet styrene as well as with the kit's side and rear vision ports and the 37 mm gun and its mantlet, Fig. 7.

Hull details. I hollowed the lights and added stretched-sprue cables. Brush guards for the lights, as well as fender supports, are made of .010" strip (Fig. 8). I filled grab-handle holes and fitted stretched-sprue handles and a front step made of .010" strip.

Replacing the kit-supplied air cleaners, I installed new ones made from ¼" styrene tubing with stretched-sprue brackets. Note how the rear storage boxes follow the slope of the rear deck; I shortened them. The soft metal of a toothpaste tube makes good straps; the buckles are stretched sprue.

Tamiya's kit replicates a diesel-powered M3, but most M3A1s had a gas engine, so I

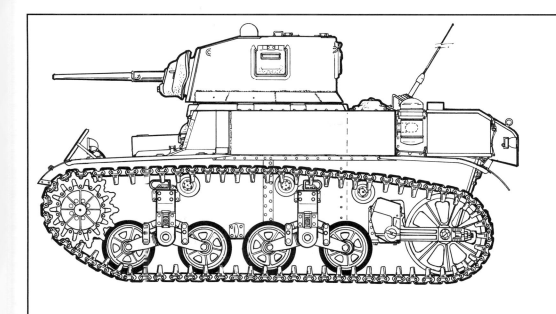

PREPARED FOR
FINESCALE MODELER
BY
RON PONIATOWSKI

1/35 SCALE

Drawings in FINESCALE MODELER may be copied for your own use only. To convert these drawings to other modeling scales, make copies at the following percentages:

1/48 - 73%

1/72 - 48.6%

1/76 - 46%

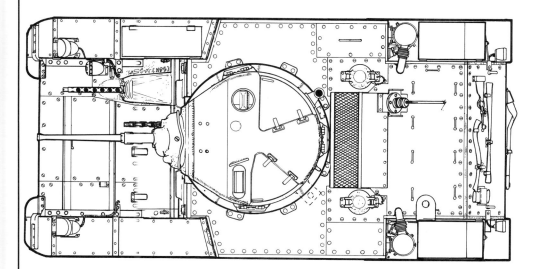

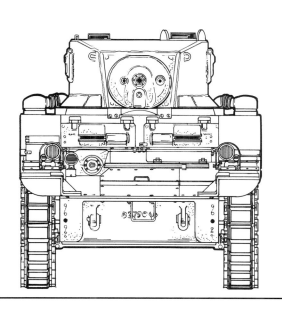

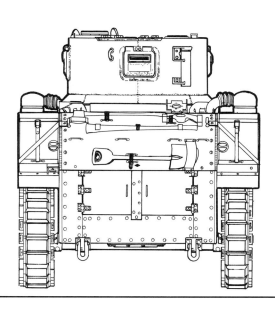

rerouted the intake hoses. Figure 9 shows the difference.

Paint and markings. I painted an overall coat of Tamiya olive drab mixed with a little Tamiya dark gray and weathered with various shades of olive, carrying the lower hull colors throughout the rest of the hull. Flowing a wash of Polly S earth yellow into cracks and around details replicated dust. When the paint dried I was ready to mark my tank as a member of the 3rd Platoon, Company C, 1st Battalion, 1st Armored Division.

The most difficult part of the markings was the 48-star American flag. I suffered through a long and expensive photoetching attempt, generating a positive image of the flag on my computer and converting it to negative film to make a photoetched mask. It didn't work—I painted the flag by hand.

After painting the entire area of the flag white, I masked the white with 3M striping tape to paint the red stripes and blue field. Finally, I used what was left of the photoetched copper plate as a mask to paint the stars, which at least saved me the trouble of painting 96 white dots. (Here's where research can save you hours of labor—I discovered later that many tanks in the same unit wore no such flags!)

The turret's yellow band is also hand painted. (The band was probably hand painted by the crew, so I didn't worry about perfect edges.) I cut the star from masking tape which I then used as

a stencil. The number within the star, as well as the fender number, are hand painted.

Casting plays a role. As my Stuart neared completion I turned toward the final exterior details, stowing modified Combat Series tools on the hull and casting other items in Alumilite, an easy-to-use casting resin.

Using a Verlinden .30 caliber machine gun as a master, I created a silicone mold and cast four machine gun barrels. I cast spare tracks for hull stowage in the same way, using kit-supplied tracks as masters.

Special thanks. I can't close without thanking the Dunellen, New Jersey, American Legion for letting me climb all over its M5. Also, thanks to the Dunellen police officer who answered that frantic call about a tank-climbing, trespassing terrorist!

SOURCES
• Alumilite: Bare-Metal Foil & Hobby, P.O. Box 82, Farmington, MI 48332
• Detail parts: Combat Series, 7070 N. Harrison, Pinedale, CA 93650
• Sheet styrene tube, rod, strip, and sheet: Plastruct, 1020 S. Wallace Place, City of Industry, CA 91748
• Scale Scenics aluminum HO scale fencing (part no. 652-3500): available from Wm. K. Walthers, P.O. Box 18676, Milwaukee, WI 53218

REFERENCE
• Zaloga, Steve, Stuart *U.S. Light Tanks in Action*, Squadron/Signal, Carollton, Texas, 1979

M3A1 STUART LIGHT TANK

Introduced in 1941, the M3A1 was the second model in the Stuart line of light tanks, incorporating combat-inspired improvements on the original M3. Internal changes included a gyro-stabilizer for better firing on the move, power turret traverse, and a turret basket. The turret silhouette was lowered by replacing a single raised hatch with two flush-fitting hatches. Two periscopes were added and the location of the left-side vision block was altered.

The hull was also upgraded. Combat experience demonstrated that an enemy round need not pierce the hull to be dangerous; inside the hull, a blown rivet could be lethal. The M3A1 reduced the number of rivets by combining riveted and welded plates. Sponsons and the rear overhang were welded. However, production overlapped and some M3A1s appeared with fully riveted hulls.

The Continental 7-cylinder, air-cooled gasoline-fueled radial engine powered most M3A1s, but 211 of them had Guibertson diesel engines. Externally, you could tell the difference by the air filter hoses; diesels had longer hoses.

By October 1943 American Car and Foundry had produced 13,859 M3s, of which 4,621 were M3A1s.

MODELING THE MAXSON-STUART ANTIAIRCRAFT TANK

A simple conversion produces an experimental prototype in 1/35 scale

BY TERRY SUNDAY

In 1942, the United States Army Ordnance Department developed several experimental prototypes for air defense vehicles. One design started with the reliable M3 Stuart light tank, which had been produced at the American Car & Foundry Company since March 1941. In service at the time with both the U.S. and British armies, the Stuart was the most widely used American-built light tank.

The prototype "Maxson-Stuart" air defense vehicle com-bined a standard M3 hull and running gear with an M45 Maxson power turret. The Maxson turret mounted four Browning M2 .50 caliber machine guns.

Although the diminutive Maxson-Stuart performed wall in mobility and firing trials, it wasn't put into production. Instead, the Army perfected a competing design, the General Motors Corporation T58, which used the same Maxson turret mounted in the armored cargo bed of an M3 half-track. The result, accepted by the service and put into production, was the Gun Motor Carriage M16.

This conversion depicts the Maxson-Stuart as it might have appeared had it been produced and deployed during World War Two. The basic model is a straightforward replica of the prototype, based on a single photograph in the August 1987 issue of the Japanese magazine *Panzer*. I extrapolated here and there to model the one-of-a-kind test prototype as a production-type combat vehicle.

The model. The project uses two 1/35 scale Tamiya kits, the M3

Terry's model is a might-have-been antiaircraft system based on one prototype actually built.

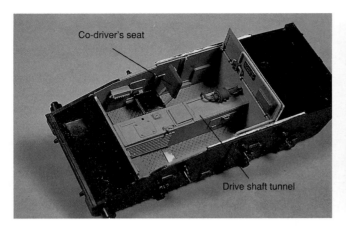

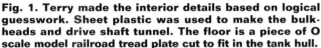

Fig. 1. Terry made the interior details based on logical guesswork. Sheet plastic was used to make the bulkheads and drive shaft tunnel. The floor is a piece of O scale model railroad tread plate cut to fit in the tank hull.

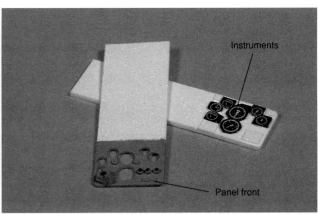

Fig. 2. The instrument panel was made by sandwiching Waldron instruments into a front panel.

Stuart (No. 3542) and the M16 Multiple Gun Motor Carriage (No. MM-181A). I used the Maxson turret plus a few other odds and ends from the M16 kit. This may seem a waste, but the rest of the halftrack kit remains nearly intact for later use. You could make a Maxson-Stuart model simply by attaching the M16's turret to the Stuart hull; however, if you're a superdetailing fan as I am, there is room for improvement.

Interior details. Lacking detailed information about the interior, I relied on general armored vehicle knowledge, common sense, and what well-known modeler Sheperd Paine calls "creative gizmology." Very little of the interior is visible, as the only opening is the driver's hatch, so I concentrated on detailing the near sides of the interior that can be seen through the open hatch.

I mounted all the interior parts in a lower hull tub, test fitting the upper hull often to make sure there wasn't any interference. A piece of O scale model railroad tread plate formed the bottom of the crew compartment,

with .040" sheet plastic bulkheads front and rear. The rear bulkhead lines up with rivets molded on the outer hull.

I made a drive shaft tunnel from sheet plastic, running between the rear-mounted air-cooled engine and forward-mounted transmission. I don't know if the Stuart had such a tunnel, but it seemed reasonable to shield the heavy, rotating drive shaft that passed through the crew compartment. Added details included inspection and access plates, reinforcing ribs, bolt heads, and driver's controls (Fig. 1).

Using an adaptation of the sandwich techniques described in "Detailing Aircraft Cockpits" (Fall 1983 FSM), I made the driver's instrument panel. The dial faces came from a 1/32 scale Waldron German WWII aircraft instrument set. I cut out individual dials and glued them to the backing plate, lining each up with a matching hole drilled in the instrument panel itself (Fig. 2). Since the instrument faces were already glossy, I left out the thin piece of transparent plastic that normally is a part of the sandwich.

Filler putty applied around the edges eliminated the layered look. I detailed the panel with bolt heads, lights, switches, and placards, then mounted it inside the driver's hatch opening in the upper hull.

The interior of any armored vehicle is crowded with wires, junction boxes, brackets, cables, and other equipment. Using pieces of solder, plastic rod, sections of square and flat plastic strip, bolt heads, and parts from my scrap box, I added clutter to the crew compartment. Again, I put most of the effort into those areas visible through the driver's hatch. Some of the cables, for example, end abruptly on the right side of the drive shaft tunnel.

The driver's and co-driver's seats came from the M16 kit. I reasoned that an operational Maxson-Stuart probably would have had a crew of three, so I included a folding jump seat on the rear bulkhead for the gunner when he wasn't in the turret. I made the driver's pedals, steering levers, and gearshift from plastic strip (Fig. 3). The driver's seat belt—the only one that can be seen—was made

Fig. 3. The driver's seat and levers were mounted on a thin piece of plastic and handled as a separate subassembly.

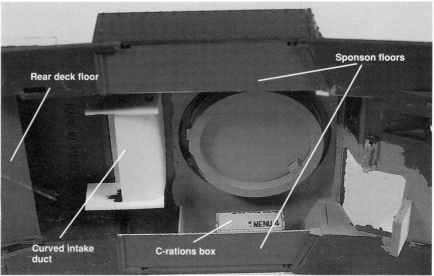

Rear deck floor

Sponson floors

Curved intake duct

C-rations box

MENU 4

Fig. 4. Plastic sheet floors were added under the sponsons and rear deck overhand. Note the curved air intake duct mounted under the rear deck to prevent seeing through and the Verlinden C-ration box in the left sponson.

from Chartpak graphics tape with Waldron buckles. The co-driver's bow machine gun, with the barrel drilled out, came from Tamiya's U.S. Infantry Weapons Set (No. MM-221).

Hull detailing. Tamiya's M3 hull is nicely done, faithfully reproducing the Stuart's distinctive riveted and bolted armor panels. However, like nearly all Tamiya kits, there were gaping holes where the sponsons were. I filled these holes with .010" sheet plastic and filled the equally gaping hole beneath the rear deck overhang with .040" plastic. Since the insides of the sponsons would be barely visible through the driver's hatch, I added rear bulkheads which lined up with rows of rivets on the upper hull. A radio, ammo cans, a box of Verlinden C rations, and other miscellaneous equipment filled out the details (Fig. 4).

A bit of surgery on the upper deck was required. I cut out the molded intake and replaced the solid rear half with a new part made from .010" plastic. I built a curved intake duct, painted it flat black, and mounted it inside the hull below the cutout (Fig. 4). This prevents seeing through to the bottom of the hull. I then covered the remaining intake area with fine stainless-steel grille, cut and bent to the proper shape.

I carefully cut out the driver's two hatch doors, one on the glacis plate and one in the hull front. These were thinned down and detailed with latches, braces, vision block mounts, and bolt heads on their inner surfaces (Fig. 5).

The Stuart's turret mounting ring was a little oversize for the base of the Maxson turret (M16 part No. C19). To make a tight fit, I cut .010" x .125" plastic strip long enough to encircle the turret base twice. I wrapped it tightly

Fig. 5. The driver's hatches were cut out, thinned down, and detailed on the inner side, which shows when they are opened.

Plastic strip spacers

Fig. 6. Strip plastic wrapped around the turret base built up the circumference so the base would fit tightly into the M3 turret ring. A smaller strip created a ledge.

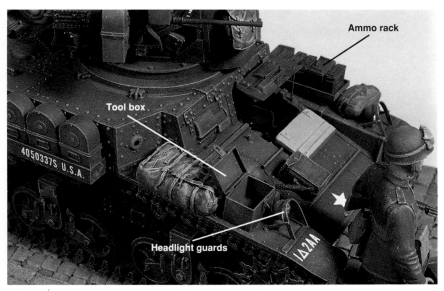

Fig. 8. Terry filled in the open backs of the M16 kit ammunition drums. Then he sanded them smooth and added ribs.

Fig. 7. A storage rack for small-arms ammo was added to the left front fender in front of the sponson; the right fender received an opened toolbox. The rounded hull machine gun mount was made from the end of a CONTAC capsule cut off, with a hole for the machine gun added. New headlights were made from M. V. Products' model railroad lenses, and headlight guards were scratchbuilt from plastic strip.

around my X-acto knife handle, giving it permanent bend, then glued the curved strip around the turret base. A second narrow strip, glued just above the first (Fig. 6), positioned the turret base vertically so the turret itself would just clear the M3's top deck.

I assumed the Maxson-Stuart would not have had the M3's twin sponson-mounted .30 caliber machine guns. These guns were of limited use and were frequently removed by combat crews; they disappeared entirely from the M3A1 and later variants. I used the spaces in front of the sponsons for storage, adding a small-arms ammo can rack to the left fender and a small toolbox to the right fender (Fig. 7).

I drilled out the kit headlights and added M. V. Products' clear model locomotive lenses. The kit headlight guards were thick, so I replaced them with scratchbuilt substitutes made from .010" strip plastic (Fig. 7). Getting both the

angle and size right at the same time was a trial-and-error process, and I threw away many pieces before finally getting good parts.

An operational air defense vehicle needs ample supplies of ammunition and fuel, so I built racks for eight .50 caliber ammunition drums, four on each sponson. The

drums came from the M16 kit; their open backs were filled with pieces of square plastic strip and putty (Fig. 8).

A gas can rack was built from .010" plastic sheet and .010" x .125" strip and mounted in place of the standard M3's right rear hull storage box. Tie-down strap attachments, the strap (made with Chartpak tape and Waldron buckles), and four Italeri gas cans were added to complete the rack (Fig. 9).

I re-created the Stuart's unique angled radio antenna mounting bracket using tiny pieces

Fig. 9. The unique angled antenna mount was made from plastic and the air intake screen from stainless steel mesh.

of plastic strip and bolt heads. The antenna base was from Verlinden Products, and a piece of thin brass wire, attached with super glue, served as the antenna (Fig. 9).

I also converted the vehicle from diesel to gasoline power. Unmodified, Tamiya's kit represents a diesel-engined M3, recognized by long pipes running from the sides of the cooling air intake to the air filters. On the gasoline version, the pipes were shorter and entered the rear deck behind the cooling air intake. I made the conversion with thick plastic rod, cut and joined in a 90-degree bend (Fig. 9).

The kit's road wheels, suspension, and tracks were well detailed so no additional work was necessary. Because the suspension would be under a lot of strain with tight tracks, I used plenty of liquid cement to attach the parts and allowed extra drying time before installing the tracks.

Turret detailing. The M16's Maxson turret, although well detailed straight from the box, was also a candidate for improvement. My reference was a trailer-mounted version of the same turret on display at the Air Defense Museum at Fort Bliss in E1 Paso, Texas. A few Polaroid photos provided all the information I needed.

My turret detailing mainly involved adding small parts until the overall effect looked authentic. I added battery cables and hold-down bolts, a spark plug wire for the small one-cylinder engine, and an electrical junction box. Liberal use of miscellaneous scrap parts, plastic strip stock, CalScale model railroad components, and bolt heads created an appropriate look-

Fig. 10. The finished model was mounted on a Verlinden cobblestone base with a figure, a duffel bag, and an ammo can added to inject life into the scene.

ing amount of detail. Most of the extra detailing can't be seen—it's hidden under the gunner's seat and behind the engine and battery.

A new gunner's firing control box was made by adapting handles from the machine guns in Tamiya's Pink Panther Land Rover kit. I also drilled out the barrels of the four .50 caliber machine guns from the M16 kit. Two Verlinden tank crew bags, hanging from a rope on the front shield, completed the tiny but intricate turret.

Finishing touches. During assembly, I painted the subassemblies (hull, running gear, and turret) Humbrol Olive Drab. Then a black wash, followed by lighter Olive Drab dry-brushing brought out the surface textures and emphasized the many tiny details. Verlinden dry transfers were used for the national insignia and unit markings. Finally, I added several Verlinden resin-cast parts to produce the appearance of an operational combat vehicle, rather than a test prototype. Rolled and folded tarps on the deck, crew

equipment stowage bags, and ammo cans all enhanced the image of a well-used vehicle.

The base is a 5" x 7" wood decoupage plaque, stained dark walnut. I cut a resin Verlinden cobblestone street slightly smaller than the plaque (yes, a lot of the street was wasted), and glued it in place. I masked the exposed wood and airbrushed the street section Humbrol medium gray. The usual black wash and dry-brushing techniques brought out detail in the cobblestones. To add life to the scene, I placed a Verlinden figure, a duffel bag, and storage box—actually a 20 mm ammo can (Fig. 10)—on the street in front of the vehicle.

SOURCES
• Cal-Scale, P.O. Box 322, Montoursville, PA 17754
• M. V. Products, P.O. Box 6622, Orange, CA 92667
•Verlinden Productions, Lone Star Industrial Park, 811 Lone Star Drive, O'Fallon, MO 63366
• Photoetched detail parts: Waldron Model Products, P.O. Box 431, Merlin, OR 97532

M728 COMBAT ENGINEER VEHICLE

Pick your Patton and go to work!

BY ANDREW CRUTCHLEY

You can usually find several 1/35 scale M60 Patton tank kits, but what about an M728 combat engineer vehicle based on the Patton? No, you won't find that machine—but you can base it on an M60. I used an Esci 1/35 scale M60A3 (kit No. 8317).

Take care of the turret, then start with a boom. After joining the turret halves, fill the mounting points on the sides for handrails, jerry cans, and other equipment (Fig. 1). The M728 doesn't have the range-finder bulges of the M60; fill those holes, too.

Measure and mark the position of the boom's pivot-tube centers. Be precise; errors here will be magnified as the boom takes shape. Slowly drill small holes, then enlarge them with a round file to 13/64" (5 mm) diameter.

Figure 2 shows the components of the boom as well as other scratchbuilt parts. For boom mounts, cut 13/64" brass tubing to length according to the scale drawings on page 76, clean up the cut ends, and epoxy the tubing in the turret, being extra careful of alignment. Create the weld beads around the turret-tube joint with Milliput or a similar epoxy putty.

The boom's A frame is made from 5/32" and 1/8" styrene rod. Copy the scale drawings and mount them on cardboard with

Need something moved? Try an M728. If you can't roll over it, push it down, or tow it away, you can always blow it up with the 165 mm gun!

3M Spray Mount. Build the boom on the copy, tacking the rods in place on the plans as you glue them together. Let the boom assembly dry thoroughly before removing it from the plans.

About 1/2" from the boom pivot is a double-flanged joint (Fig. 1). Cut two rings (1/4" outside diameter and 5/32" inside) from .040" sheet styrene, position them on the boom, and add eight bolt heads to each side of the flange. Use stretched sprue and

wire to add J hooks, hook eyes, and grab handles.

Reeling in the cable, raising the boom. Check your spares box for an eight-spoke pulley wheel for the top of the boom (Figs. 2 and 3). Make a cable guide from scrap plastic. The guide—two right angles joined at their open ends by two small rollers—pivots on the pulley-wheel axle (Fig. 3).

Use scrap plastic for other details, too. Make the Y-shaped cable stay for the top of the boom;

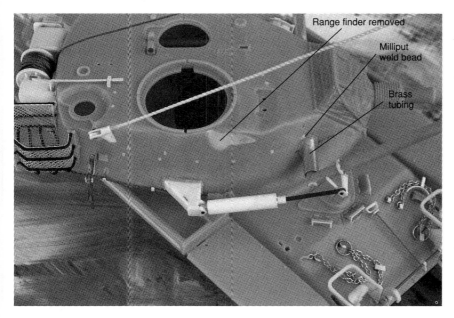

Range finder removed

Milliput weld bead

Brass tubing

Fig. 1. One of the first steps is to fill unneeded holes in the turret—not all the M60 equipment is needed. The boom mount is brass tubing.

On the right side of the turret below the cupola is the hydraulic strut which moves the boom (Fig. 4). Make it from 3/16" styrene tubing, mount 3/32" tubing inside that, and fashion a rubber boot. Make a 1"-long piston from .040" rod, flattening one end of the rod for the attachment point. Join two plastic triangles to form the piston-rod pivot.

The snatch block is a pulley wheel sandwiched between two pear-shaped plates with shackles at the wide end for attaching cables or chains. It's usually stowed on the turret next to the left boom pivot. Make it from .020" sheet styrene and plastic scraps (Fig. 5).

Winding up the winch. The winch assembly comprises a cable drum, two hydraulic-motor housings, and a control lever, Figs. 2 and 6. The drum is a 9/32"-long section of 9/32" tubing. Make dished ends for the drum from

this also pivots on the pulley-wheel axle (Figs. 2 and 3). Attached to the Y-frame base is a diamond-shaped cross member: Attach this to the Y frame, and the two cable stays to either end.

Anchor the ends of the cable on the turret sides (Fig. 4). Just below these anchors are the boom's travel locks. The clamps are identical to the rear-deck-mounted gun lock on an M60.

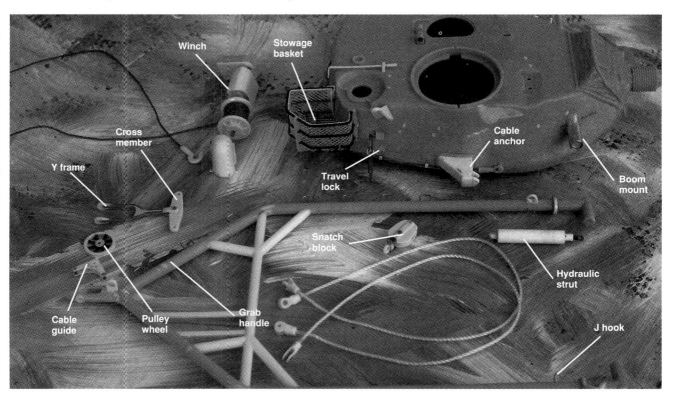

Winch

Stowage basket

Cross member

Y frame

Cable guide

Pulley wheel

Grab handle

Snatch block

Travel lock

Cable anchor

Boom mount

Hydraulic strut

J hook

Fig. 2. Here's a look at the boom, winch, and other M728 equipment before installation.

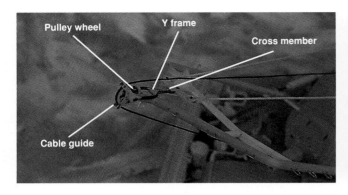

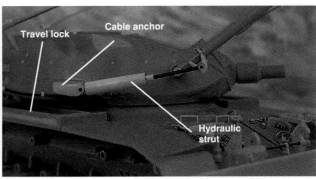

Fig. 3. The pulley-wheel assembly tops off the boom.

Fig. 4. Turret-mounted anchors secure the cable; travel locks hold the boom. The struts are styrene tubing.

The author enhanced Verlinden's M9 'dozer blade; if it's not green or tan, it's an add-on part.

.040" styrene sheet. Add an .040" x ⁵⁄₃₂" disk to the center of each drum end and glue eight triangular spokes between the central boss and the drum ends.

The motor housings are ⁵⁄₁₆"-thick laminated plastic blocks, filed and sanded to fit the turret surface. Use stretched sprue for a winch control lever between the right winch mount and cupola. Add the jerry can and holder (made from sheet scraps) to the end of the left winch mount.

The stowage basket for the turret is smaller than the M60 basket because of the winch. Glue an .040" sheet-styrene mount on the turret's right side below the ventilator and form the frame from .040" rod. About halfway around the basket is a support—I used a

Fig. 7. Styrene tubing or a modified kit part can provide the short-barreled demolition gun.

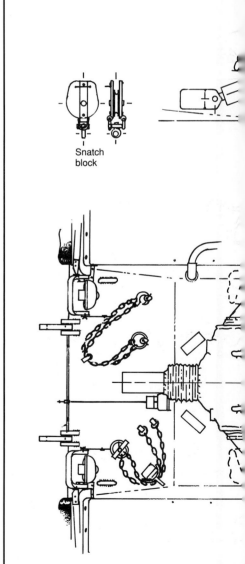

Snatch block

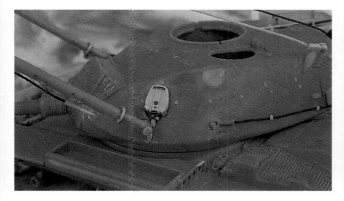

Fig. 5. Andrew made a snatch block from .020" sheet styrene and plastic scraps.

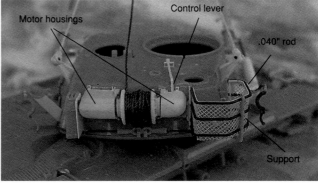

Motor housings

Control lever

.040" rod

Support

Fig. 6. Reeling in the details: The scratchbuilt winch and stowage basket take their places at the turret rear. Andrew sanded the motor housings to fit the turret surface.

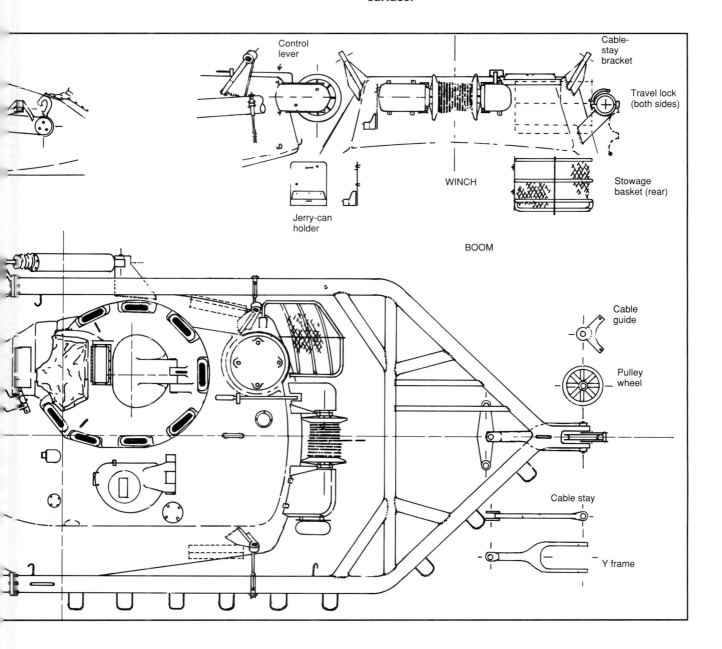

Control lever

Cable-stay bracket

Travel lock (both sides)

WINCH

Stowage basket (rear)

Jerry-can holder

BOOM

Cable guide

Pulley wheel

Cable stay

Y frame

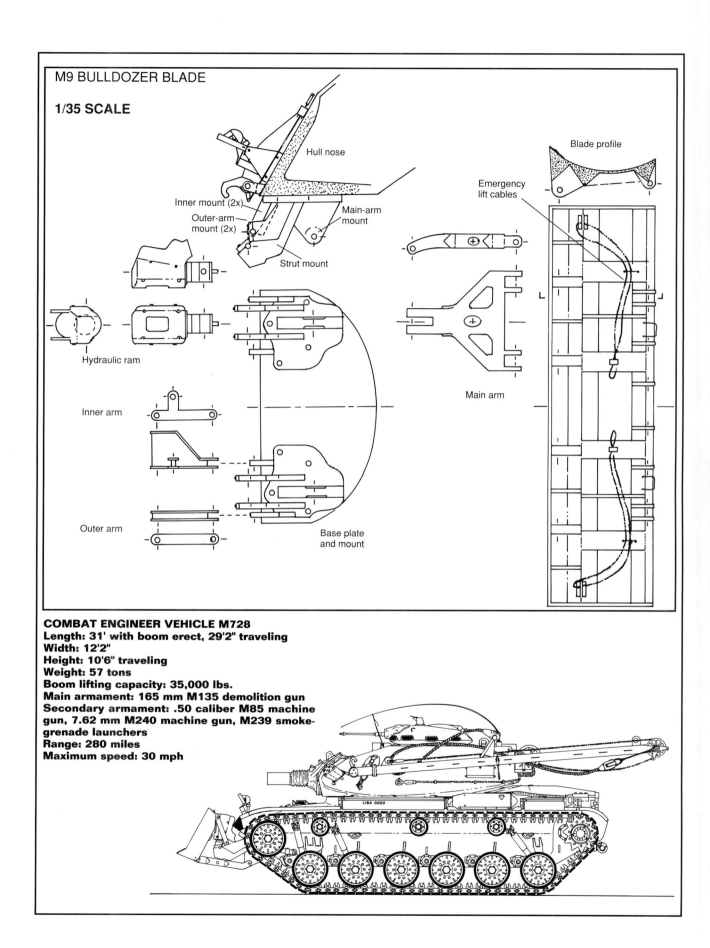

M9 BULLDOZER BLADE

1/35 SCALE

Hull nose

Inner mount (2x)

Outer-arm mount (2x)

Main-arm mount

Strut mount

Hydraulic ram

Inner arm

Outer arm

Base plate and mount

Blade profile

Emergency lift cables

Main arm

COMBAT ENGINEER VEHICLE M728
Length: 31' with boom erect, 29'2" traveling
Width: 12'2"
Height: 10'6" traveling
Weight: 57 tons
Boom lifting capacity: 35,000 lbs.
Main armament: 165 mm M135 demolition gun
Secondary armament: .50 caliber M85 machine gun, 7.62 mm M240 machine gun, M239 smoke-grenade launchers
Range: 280 miles
Maximum speed: 30 mph

USA 0000

kit part, merely locating it differently. Replicate the mesh with tulle (bridal veil) Use kit-supplied tow cables and eyes, but note how the cable is strung.

Demolition gun, bits and pieces. The 165 mm M135 demolition gun is simply made. Keep only the concertina section of the kit-supplied gun parts and make a new gun tube from $13/32$"-long $7/32$" tubing. The Esci M60 wading trunks are the right diameter; merely bore out the tube to $3/16$" (Fig. 7).

Use spare parts for exterior details such as lifting eyes, cupola, hatches, turret blower, searchlight cable duct, and antenna bases. Fit the AN/VSS-1 or AN/VSS-3 searchlight depending on whether it's an early- or late-model M60, respectively. Many M728s have M239 smoke-grenade launchers mounted in front of the boom

pivot with the ammunition boxes mounted near the boom lock.

M9 bulldozer blade. The blade is a permanent fixture; all the controls, pumps, reservoir, and pipes are inside the tank. You could scratchbuild it by thermoforming styrene and build the rest of the structure with styrene rod and tubing. But shortcuts are available in the form of the Verlinden or I-Corps M9 'dozer blade; I used the former. The drawings and photos on pages 76 and 77 show the blade as well as the kit I used. You can embellish it with two emergency lift cables and grab handles.

Paint, weathering, and stowage. The CEV M728 has been in service since 1968, so you have choices for color schemes. I chose to "station" mine in California in the early 1980s. It sports a gray-desert scheme of sand (FS30277),

field drab (FS30118), earth yellow (FS30257), and black.

Paint the gun mantlet and cupola machine-gun dust covers faded olive drab with a heavy dry-brushing of sand. Dry-brush the blade with silver to replicate exposed metal under worn paint, then dry-brush again with reddish brown for rust.

Add a heavy coat of dust, especially on rear horizontal surfaces where dirt is kicked up by the tracks. Dirt also accumulates in creases as well as oil and fuel spills near the fuel caps and engine-deck access grilles and hatches. Rear vertical grilles are always stained by exhaust.

This vehicle can be decorated with crew bags, tarps, boxes, jerry cans, and other external stowage. When it's lowered for travel, the boom is ideal for storage!

COMBAT ENGINEER VEHICLE M728

World War II demonstrated the usefulness of armored engineer vehicles for construction, demolition, and tank recovery. After the war the U.S. Army planned to base an all-purpose engineer vehicle on whatever main battle tank succeeded the M4 Sherman.

The first plans were for the M26 Pershing tank. The design shifted to the M46 Patton in 1948, with a British 165 mm T156 demolition gun mounted in the turret. This vehicle featured an adapted M3 bulldozer blade, a winch, an A-frame boom on the rear deck, and an emergency boom on the front. The design was adapted as other tanks were approved by the Army, until the equipment came to rest on the

M60A1 hull and turret in 1960.

In its late developmental stages the engineer vehicle was designated T118E1. The T156 gun had been replaced with the 165 mm M135, range-finder ports of the M60 turret were deleted, and a hydraulic A-frame boom was mounted near the front of the turret. The boom, an M9 'dozer blade, and a turret-mounted, two-speed, 25,000-pound winch were operated from inside the vehicle. The M9 blade also was developed as a depot retrofit for M60 tanks in the field.

Chrysler built the M728 at the Detroit Tank Arsenal, starting in 1963. It entered service in 1965, seeing action in Vietnam and continuing through Desert Storm. The M728 still serves the United States as well as Saudi Arabia and Singapore. More than 300 have been produced.

REFERENCES
Hunnicutt, R. P., *Patton: A History of the American Main Battle Tank*, Presidio Press, Novato, California, 1984
Mesko, Jim, *M60 Patton in Action*, Squadron/Signal Publications, Carrollton, Texas, 1986

SOURCES
• Styrene sheet, rod, and tube: Evergreen Scale Models, 12808 N. E. 125th Way, Kirkland, WA 98034
• Brass tubing: K&S Engineering, 6917 W. 59th St., Chicago, IL 60638
• Milliput: Verlinden Productions, Lone Star Industrial Park, 811 Lone Star Drive, O'Fallon, MO 63366
• M9 bulldozer blades: Verlinden Productions (address above), I-Corps Model Co., 3317 W. Bottsford Ave., Greenfield, WI 53221-2135

BUILDING A PANZER IV/70 (A) IN 1/35 SCALE

This straightforward conversion could be your first taste of kitbashing

Kitbashing is the art of combining pieces from one kit with pieces from another to produce a different and unique model. Here, Dan combines MRC-Tamiya's Panzer IV Ausf H and Jagdpanzer IV L/70 Lang to form the Interim Panzer IV/70 (A).

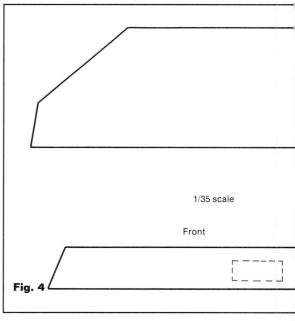

1/35 scale

Front

Fig. 4

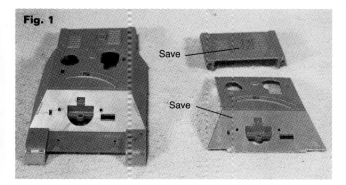

Fig. 1

Save

Save

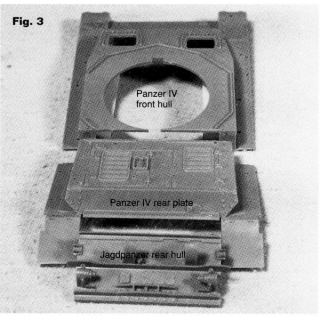

Fig. 3

Panzer IV front hull

Panzer IV rear plate

Jagdpanzer rear hull

Fig. 2

Relocated roller

Remove

BY DAN TISONCIK

Germany used many different vehicles as tank destroyers during World War Two. To meet the ever-increasing demand, several nonstandard designs were produced in limited numbers.

The Panzer IV/70 (A) was built on an unaltered PzKpfw IV chassis with a superstructure similar to that of the Panzer IV/70 (V), but higher. The lower superstructure was vertical and had a visor for the driver. The gun was mounted in the front sloped superstructure and had a 10-degree traverse range. It was held at a 13-degree elevation by a travel lock when moving in noncombat areas.

The weight of the longer gun made the vehicle nose heavy, so the first four wheels on each side were steel rimmed to reduce wear on the normal rubber wheels. Secondary armament on late models included the "von Satz P" mount in the roof over the gunner. This was a 7.92 mm machine gun with a curved barrel attachment. The vehicle was usually fitted with "Schürzen" (side skirt) armor that protected the sides and tracks from hollow charge projectiles (bazookas). Only 278 of this variant were built.

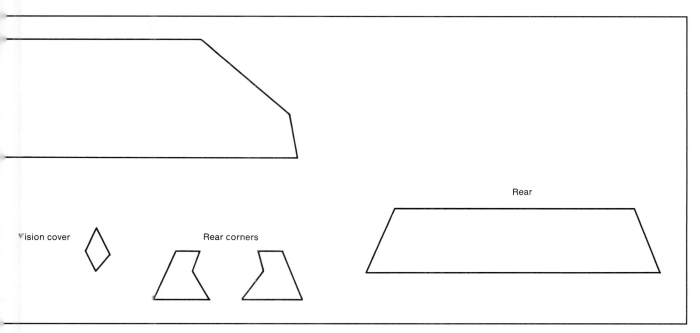

Vision cover

Rear corners

Rear

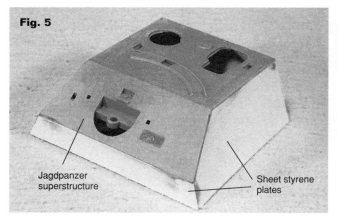

Fig. 5

Jagdpanzer superstructure

Sheet styrene plates

Fig. 6

Panzer IV front hull

Filled vision port

Jagdpanzer chassis, rear hull, and superstructure

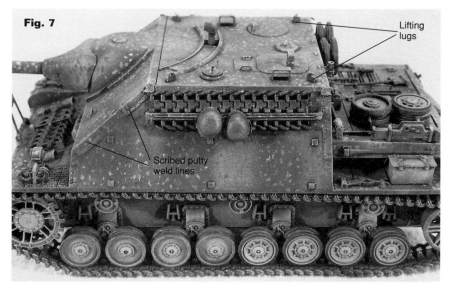

Fig. 7

Lifting lugs

Scribed putty weld lines

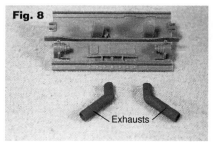

Fig. 8

Exhausts

Cut and splice. You'll need two kits to complete this conversion: Tamiya's Panzerkampfwagen IV Ausf H (No. 3554) and Jagdpanzer IV L/70 Lang (No. 3588). Start by cutting out the Jagdpanzer superstructure front and top (Fig. 1). Also cut off the rear engine deck from the remaining upper hull. Remove the two middle return rollers on each side of the chassis and replace one, centrally located between the remaining two (Fig. 2). Remove the Panzer IV engine deck (Fig. 3). Glue the rear section of the Jagdpanzer to the Panzer IV upper hull, then join the upper hull assembly to the Jagdpanzer chassis. Make the rear plate of the Panzer IV per the instructions,

leaving off the exhaust parts, and glue this section to the hull rear.

Superstructure. Cut new side and rear hull plates to complete the superstructure conversion from .040" sheet styrene using the full-size templates (Fig. 4). Trim the plates to fit the Jagdpanzer superstructure section and glue the plates in place, forming a box (Fig. 5). Fill gaps with putty, sand, and fit this new superstructure over the old Panzer IV upper hull section (Fig. 6). Place the Panzer IV driver's visor (No. C25) on the new superstructure and fill in the old Jagdpanzer vision port (Fig. 6). Cut a new gun port cover for the left side and glue the rear aerial mount to the left side of the rear superstructure.

Add lifting lugs at the upper corners of the fighting compartment (Fig. 7), and scribe putty with a hot knife to simulate weld seams at the superstructure corners.

Exhausts and suspension. Make exhausts from 35 mm-diameter aluminum tubing coated with fine-grained dental resin powder to simulate a rusted, oxidized texture (Fig. 8); any fine powder applied while the paint is still wet will do.

Mount the exhausts to the Panzer IV rear hull parts (No. C62 and C63). Scratchbuild the barrel clamp from styrene rod and strip and detail it with Grandt Line bolts (Fig. 9).

The drive sprockets, return rollers, and rear bogies are standard Panzer IV type, but use the earlier idler wheels provided in the Panzer IV kit (Nos. D2 and D8). Convert the eight front bogies to steel-rimmed wheels using the leftover rear Panzer IV/Jagdpanzer bogies. Turn them inside out, glue together, cut off the center

Fig. 9

Vision port

Barrel clamp

Fig. 10

Reworked front wheels

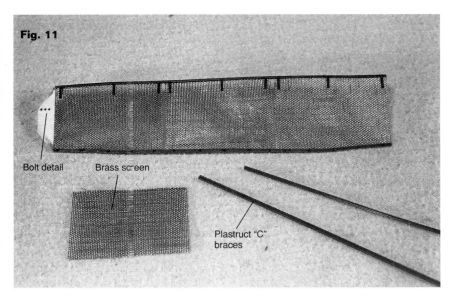

Fig. 11

Bolt detail

Brass screen

Plastruct "C" braces

molding on the front side, and sand it flush with the wheel. Then, cut the molded center disk out of the remaining front set of bogies, sand down the disks, and glue them in place (Fig. 10).

Fine details. This version of the Jagdpanzer was fitted with wire mesh "Schürzen" (side armor). Cut six (three for each side) 30 mm x 40 mm pieces from No. 50 mesh brass wire screen. Add Plastruct braces and Grandt Line bolt detail (Fig. 11). Make mounting support rods from .020"-diameter aluminum tube and supports from .010" styrene strips

(Fig. 12). Position equipment such as tools, cable, and extra tracks using photos as reference.

I painted the model in a late-war ambush camouflage scheme of sand, green, and red-brown, with contrasting spots on the hull sides and rear. No unit markings appear on this model, as was typical for late-war German vehicles.

This conversion is simple and produces a nice-looking model of a little-known Jadgpanzer IV. A. E. F. Designs now offers a resin conversion kit for this version if you prefer that alternative.

SOURCES
• A. E. F. Designs, 14413 E. 47 Ave., Denver, CO 80239
• Bolt heads: Grandt Line Products, Inc., 1040B Shary Court, Concord, CA 94518
• Tubing: K&S Engineering, 6917 W. 59th St., Chicago, IL 60638
• Plastruct, 1020 S. Wallace Place, City of Industry, CA 91748

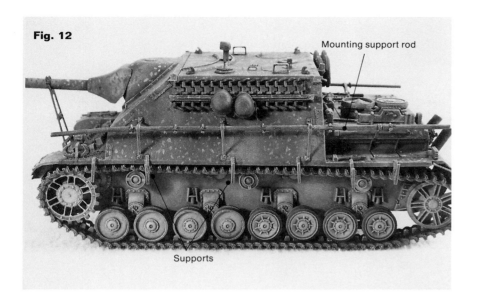

Fig. 12

Mounting support rod

Supports

PANZERJÄGER TO JAGDPANZER

Panzerjäger (tank hunter) was a weapon used to seek out and destroy enemy armor. This ranged from the 70-ton "Jagdtiger" to a single-shot, close-range Panzerfaust. Early towed antitank guns were ineffective, and eventually mobile, fully tracked, antitank weapons were developed for the German Army. The first Panzerjäger was a combination of the Panzer I Ausf B chassis and the Czech 4.7 cm gun, which replaced the tank turret.

During the 1942 Russian campaign, Russian 7.62 cm field guns were mounted in semi-open compartments on obsolete Panzer II Ausf D and E and Czech 38 (t) chassis. These early Panzerjägers had the disadvantages of high silhouettes, light armor, and minimal crew protection.

In 1942 the German long 7.5 cm antitank guns were mounted in Sturmgeschütz IIIs, producing a highly successful antitank weapon with an enclosed fighting compartment, low silhouette, and sloped armor. The Stug III served as both assault gun and tank destroyer.

Panzerjäger vehicles evolved into Jadgpanzers (hunter tanks) with the Jagdpanzer IV. Based on the Panzer IV chassis, it was intended as a replacement for the StuG III. The new design incorporated a low silhouette, sloped armor, and a long 7.5 cm gun.

The urgent requirement to mount the Panther's new high-velocity gun (75 mm L/70) in as many vehicles as possible led Adolf Hitler to order all PzKpfw IV production switched to the new Jadgpanzer IV/70. Immediate changeover wasn't possible, so Nibelungenwerke Alkett produced the interim Panzer IV/70 (A), featuring a higher superstructure on top of a standard PzKpfw IV Ausf J chassis. It was produced until the end of the war.

84

AIRBRUSHING ARMORED FIGHTING VEHICLES
Easy techniques for realistic one-color finishes

Cookie's 1/35 scale DML T72M2 shows how colorful a single-color scheme can be.

BY COOKIE SEWELL

Several years ago my daughter Katie looked over my models, decided that tanks were dull, and drew a picture of how she thought they should look: lots of red, yellow, and blue, with windows and curtains to make them cheery! Of course, there are more realistic ways to pep up single-color finishes and emphasize carefully crafted details. The correct combination of base coat and topcoat colors and airbrushing lightly produces an accurate, detailed finish. I demonstrated my techniques on DML's 1/35 scale T-72M2, which can be either Soviet khaki No. 2 (olive drab) or a lighter green.

These techniques are designed for single color schemes. If you try the same methods on two-, three-, or four-color finishes, the result will be colorful bedlam. However, you can still use my weathering and finishing suggestions.

Airbrushing. You'll need to know how to use an airbrush. I recommend either an external-mix airbrush such as the Binks Wren or Paasche H series, or an internal-mix airbrush.

Keep a bottle of thinner handy to clean the airbrush between colors, and clean it often. A few minutes invested in cleaning can save hours later. Use an artist's sketch pad for a test palette; when a sheet becomes saturated, tear it off and keep spraying. Properly thinned airbrush paint produces little over spray or back blast; too thin, it will spatter or drift.

Building to paint. Plan your construction around painting. Tanks can be built in several stages, Fig. 1. Tank hulls are usually divided neatly, and turrets are removable.

Fig. 1. Finishing from the start: Subassemblies are easier to paint.

Glue track before painting

Outer road wheels

Fig. 2. Cookie left off the road wheels to paint.

Keep subassemblies accessible to an airbrush. Remember, sprayed paint can't turn corners. Don't attach parts that will block the spray.

The hardest parts to paint are the wheels. If they are fastened with rubber collars, you can simply pull them off when you're ready to paint. Wheels with plastic retainers are more difficult. Test fit the wheels and figure out the best approach. For my T-72M2, the solution was to cement the retainers to the outer wheels and attach them later with super glue. Plastic tracks, including those with separate or grouped links, should be in place before you begin painting.

Paint stowed equipment, skirts, and other accessories separately. Use a liquid masker to cover gluing surfaces. The more subassemblies, the more "fiddly bits" to mar. Hold onto small parts by

sticking them to strips of masking tape. Attach subassemblies with slow-setting tube glue so you can pull them off and start over if you goof them up.

Tracks. Rubber-based tracks are mostly black, steel tracks are gunmetal, and combination tracks fall somewhere in between. If you are modeling a tank that has been in service for more than 24 hours, weather the tracks. I use Floquil colors such as grime, grimy black, rust, graphite, and boxcar red.

Undercoat the tracks grimy black, Fig. 3 (p. 88). Spray lightly with rust, Fig. 4. If they look too rusty or too black, neutralize the color with a light spray of grime.

Wash vinyl tracks with dish soap, then paint before installing. Let painted vinyl dry for 24 to 48 hours to minimize paint damage during installation. Be ready to touch up anyway—vinyl tracks are troublesome.

Color choices. Visit a hobby shop and ask for paint manufacturer color charts. Some shops even sell the Federal Standard FS 595 color chip collection, which provides the official U.S. shades. Never evaluate colors under fluorescent light, it skews your perception. (Ask me about my orange Nashorn sometime!)

Base coat. The trick to my painting method is the base coat. I like World War II RLM Luftwaffe colors best, especially RLM Nos. 70, 71, 72, and 73. They cover well, and the right combinations of undercoat and topcoat yields the correct final color, Fig. 5. I undercoated my T-72 with RLM No. 70, Floquil black green No. 300153, Fig. 6. I shielded the tracks from overspray with an index card.

Check hard-to-reach areas: insides of hatches and fenders,

behind and between wheels, under overhangs, and inside hinges. A thorough undercoat atones for later sins of omission. Don't accept a single color as a finished job—this is where our fun begins!

Topcoat. We're not ready to topcoat the entire model yet. Spray only the parts subjected to natural light, weather, or abrasive wear, like outer road-wheel centers, idler and drive-wheel outer faces, gun-barrel tops, flat surfaces on the turret and upper hull, and the tops of fuel tanks and stowed equipment.

Paint other surfaces only between raised lines, projections, and edges. These include the hull sides between the road wheels; gun-barrel sides between projections or straps; turret, hull, and skirt sides between external mounts; glacis plates between objects or attachments; vent and grille frames on the engine deck; stowage-bin sides; hatch centers; and areas between attachment straps. In this stage overspray is beneficial: It blends the two coats. Figure 7 shows the topcoat applied.

With one of the green RLM colors as an undercoat, U.S. AN613 olive drab (a WWII color) replicates Soviet khaki No. 2. I topcoated my tank with Floquil hunter green No. 110182, a railroad color that has since been discontinued. An equivalent would be Floquil dark green No. 300046.

Major details. Anticipating heavy weathering, I painted the skirts, tires, rubber trim, machine guns, view slits, searchlights, headlight, gun-barrel and exhaust-pipe interiors, smoke-grenade launcher caps, and laser-sight cover flat black, Fig. 8. The darker base coat keeps these objects from becoming too light when they are weathered.

The only canvas items on my

Fig. 5. PAINT CHART
Base and topcoat combinations

Color Desired	Base Coat	Topcoat
WWII U.S. olive drab	RLM 71	AN613
Modern U.S. olive drab	RLM 73	FS34087
WWII U.S. green drab	RLM 72	FS34086
Soviet khaki No. 2	FS31118	AN613
Modern Soviet green	RLM 70	Floquil hunter green
Israeli sand	FS34201	FS30277
Iraqi sand	FS34201	Humbrol F94 8th Army sand
Panzer gray	Floquil grimy black	Panzer gray
Panzer yellow	AN 615 and FS30099 (50-50 solution)	Panzer yellow

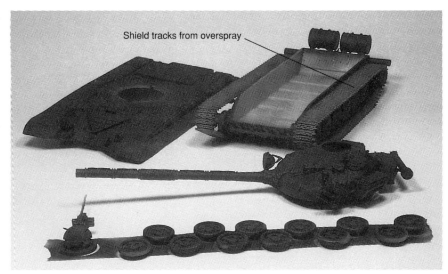

Fig. 6. The main undercoat is RLM 70, Floquil black green.

Fig. 7. A light topcoat defines details even before washes or dry-brushing.

Fig. 3. Begin the tracks with a grimy black undercoat.

Fig. 4. Next, a light spray of rust. Don't worry about overspray on the wheels—we're just getting started.

tank are the mantlet cover and the shell-casing catch bag on the machine-gun mount. I undercoated these FS31118 field drab.

Paint the exhaust and wood parts (such as machine-gun charging handles and grips and tool handles) dark brown.

Black wash. Applied selectively, a black wash deepens recesses and enhances small, molded details. Wash the depressions around wheel bolts, straps and attachments, grilles, gratings, louvers, recessed panel lines, and other major lines or edges. I used a mix-

ture of six parts Testor's Model Master airbrush thinner to one part flat-black enamel, Fig 9.

Dry-brushing. This technique makes details "snap" into view. Dry-brush all upper surfaces that are painted with the topcoat color.

Mix a 50-50 solution of light gray and the topcoat color. You can mix in a little of the dark base-coat color to replicate heavy weathering or, in the case of a light-colored vehicle, the burnishing effect of sun, wind, and sand. Dry-brushing a light color replicates sunshine on the model

surfaces. Use a wide, stiff brush. My favorite is a ½"-wide artificial-bristle brush with ⅜" bristles—in other words, a cheap brush. This lets me cover wide areas with a soft, sweeping action.

Wet the tip of the brush with paint and wipe it on a cloth rag (old T-shirts work well). Always test the brush on paper before touching the model. Figure 10 shows dry-brush strokes on my test palette. When the brush is ready, whip it lightly and rapidly across the model surface. You'll see the color build up gradually. Easy does it: The color change should be subtle. If you make a mistake, dry-brush over it with the topcoat.

Figures 11, 12, and 13 show the effects of the topcoat, wash, and dry-brushing. Who needs photoetched detail parts! Now complete the tank except for working details like the hatches and cupola.

Finish the tracks, then wax. Start with a black wash overall. To replicate track wear, dry-brush with Rub 'n Buff silver leaf and buff with a soft cloth, Fig. 14. Then glue the road wheels in place and touch them up lightly with a little of the topcoat color.

Airbrushing a clear wax overcoat makes the paint look smoother (say good-bye to lap marks on brush-painted objects). Also, wax provides a smooth surface for decals, Fig. 15.

I airbrush with Future floor wax. Applied in a fine mist, it dries almost instantly. Remember to keep a jar of water handy and shoot all of it through the airbrush immediately after finishing with wax, or the wax will clog your airbrush.

Now you're ready for decals. Use a mild setting solution: a strong solution such as Solvaset not only binds the decal to the

Field-drab undercoat

Flat black

Fig. 8. Cookie painted a few more details before applying a wash. The flat black areas will receive heavy weathering.

Fig. 9. Recesses and wrinkles appear after a flat-black wash. Look at how the mantlet changed from Fig. 8.

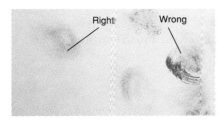

Right   Wrong

Fig. 10. Dry-brush test: The strokes on the right indicate the brush is too full. At left, the correct application.

Fig. 11. The engine deck after the base coat and topcoat have been applied.

Fig. 12. A black wash provides contrast by "deepening" recessed details.

Fig. 13. Dry-brushing highlights details, augmenting the effects of washes.

Fig. 14. Dry-brushed Rub 'n Buff replicates bare metal.

wax, it dissolves the wax and leaves nasty white streaks.

Final coats and weathering. Because we've already dry-brushed and applied a wash, our weathering is almost complete. I choose from only two or three colors as this stage: Testor's Dullcote, Floquil dust, and Floquil grimy black.

Dullcote, a clear flat lacquer, protects against nicks and fingerprints. To ensure smooth, even application, warm the bottle in hot water (110–120 F) before spraying.

Floquil dust, a clear flat, is a modeler's best friend—especially if he is married and his wife prefers clean models and shelves. You can't see the real dust and neither can she. (Warning: Modeling judges can tell the difference!) The real reason to use dust is that it's the flattest finish you can get without obscuring details.

Apply grimy black only around machine-gun ports and exhausts. Paint the lights and view ports with Micro Kristal-Kleer. Figure 16 shows one way to replicate a clear headlight: I covered an undercoat of Testor's silver with three coats of Micro Kristal-Kleer. The market lights are white, and the taillights and turn signals are Testor's turn-signal red and amber, respectively.

All that's left is to paint the figure. That's another story! Attach a stretched-sprue antenna, touch up the base, and you're ready to roll!

Fig. 15. A coat of wax smooths paint strokes and presents a smooth surface for decals.

Headlight

Fig. 16. Bright idea for headlights: One coat of Testor's silver and three coats of Micro Kristal-Kleer replicates a lens.

SOURCES
• Floquil Military colors paint series: Floquil-Polly S Color Corporation, Route 30 N., Amsterdam, NY 12010-9204
• FS595 paint-chip fan deck: Send $15 and a self-addressed label to General Services Administration, Room 6654, Attention Specifications Section 3FBP-W, 7th and D Streets SW, Washington, DC 20407
• Micro Kristal-Kleer: Microscale, P.O. Box 11950, Costa Mesa, CA 92627

A VIETNAM M3 HALF-TRACK IN 1/35 SCALE
A conversion based on Tamiya's M21

Hilber's M3 half-track is a simple conversion that results in a model representative of the early years of the Vietnam conflict. Positioned at the rear of convoys, the addition of these heavily armed vehicles made ambush a far more dangerous undertaking than before.

BY HILBER GRAF

Early in the Vietnam war, U.S. military strategists decreed that the jungle was no place for armored vehicles. American mechanized infantry was dismounted (except for the Marines, who refused to alter their operational procedures). However, the dogmatic attitudes of the MACV (Military Assistance Command, Vietnam) were eventually swayed by the protection that armor offered.

As the war took shape, the need to protect convoys from enemy hit-and-run tactics quickly became apparent. World War

Two and Korean War vehicles (some were leftovers from the French occupation of Vietnam) were hastily modified for escort duty. The ubiquitous U.S. half-track armored personnel carrier (APC) was one of these.

To upgrade war surplus mortar-carrying half-tracks, the standard 81 mm mortar was replaced by a 107 mm heavy mortar; makeshift modifications were made to accommodate the larger weapon. Other armament included M60 machine guns, and sometimes a pedestal-mounted recoilless rifle or twin .50 caliber machine guns; this mortar track could also fire canister rounds of white phosphorous or flechettes (steel darts). Individual modifications meant that no two of these APCs were alike.

The biggest obstacle to modeling this vehicle is a lack of reference material. Susceptible to mines and rocket grenades, and not nimble off the road, the half-track's Vietnam tour of duty was short-lived. Hence, there are few photographs of half-tracks in

Vietnam. Most show them in French or ARVN (Army of the Republic of Vietnam) service. I relied on my own experience with M3 half-tracks, and information supplied by a veteran who served in Vietnam during 1966.

Conversion ingredients. The model I built depicts a modified M3. Although Tamiya makes a 1/35 scale M3 (kit No. 35070), its detail is poor: It is actually easier to convert Tamiya's 1/35 scale M21 (kit No. 35083) than to clean up the M3. Additionally, I

used parts of the Tamiya 1/35 scale U.S. Infantry Weapons set, Italeri and Verlinden jerry cans, and a few minor parts from Tamiya's M557 armored command post and M3.

For scratchbuilding and detailing, you'll need: .015" and .050" sheet styrene; .020" x .080" strip styrene; Grandt Line nuts and bolts; copper lamp-cord wire and lead foil.

From the chassis up. The Tamiya chassis and drive train need little modification. Winches were

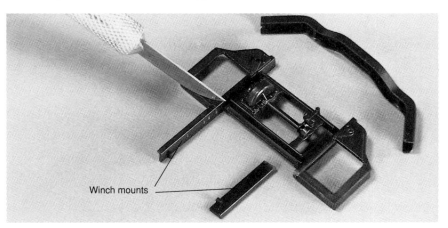

Winch mounts

Fig. 1. Winches were removed from most Vietnam half-tracks; here, the mounting bars are sliced off and the spare parts rearranged for a more accurate representation.

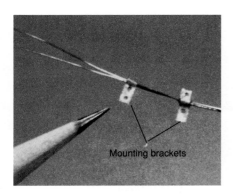

Fig. 2. Form details with lead foil—the seal on wine bottles is a good source.

commonly removed from Vietnam half-tracks, so omit the winch shaft, gear box, and roller (Tamiya kit parts C17, C25, and C30). Slice off both mounting bars from the winch guard (part C9), Fig. 1. Glue these to the chassis frame (part A1), allowing the bars to extend ¼" beyond the frame's front edge, then attach the bumper (part C26) to these supports. Glue the front hooks (parts A6) to the bumper's top edge.

Individual strands of copper wire from lamp cord make good brake lines: Drill an .0145" hole in the back of each front-wheel brake cover (parts A38) and super glue a 4" strand of wire in each

drilled hole. The brake lines run along the axle and frame and up into the engine compartment; trim the excess wire at that end. You can attach the brake lines to the frame with mounting brackets made of lead foil, Fig. 2; wrap them around the wires, then super glue them to the frame.

I made ¹⁄₁₆"-long tire valve stems from stretched sprue. Look closely at the wheel rims (parts A23): There is a small rectangular indentation near the molded lug nuts. Glue the valve stem to this spot. To simulate weight, flatten the bottom of each tire slightly with a hot knife.

Rusted mufflers. Exhaust systems rusted quickly in Southeast Asia. For realistic rust, brush liquid plastic cement on the muffler assembly (part A17), then roll the part in baking soda. Painting and weathering completes the effect. I protect painted subassemblies with plastic food wrap to prevent dust and fingerprints.

Bed construction. Skip through the Tamiya kit instructions to Step 10, regarding the bed floor. Save floor panel B (part C27), floor panel A (part C28), and the

pedestal gun mount (part C23); put the rest of the parts for this step (C6, C8, C11, C24, and C29) in your scrap box.

Figure 3 is a template for the floor: Cut it from .050" styrene, test fit, then glue it to floor panel A. Drawing a center line on the floor helps align floor details.

Carefully cut away the fuel tanks and mortar round holders from floor panel B. Repair the resulting hole in the left fuel tank by gluing the left corner mortar round holder over it. Butt and glue the large round holder to the right tank's forward wall. Align these subassemblies with the new floor edges, Fig. 4, keeping the fuel tanks in the same position as they were on the original kit, and glue them in place. Glue the remaining round holder on the floor's right front corner. Use filler putty to smooth gaps.

For the mortar stays, cut .020" x .080" strip styrene and glue it in the position indicated by the floor template. Slice off the carrying handles of the 107 mm mortar base (part Z8) and glue the base ⅝" behind the mortar stay. Cut a mounting plate for the gun

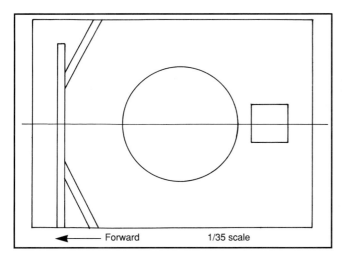

Fig. 3. FLOOR TEMPLATE

Forward   1/35 scale

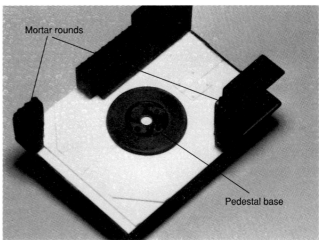

Mortar rounds

Pedestal base

Fig. 4. Floor details: Mortar rounds are cut to fit, and a base for the gun pedestal is glued to the new floor.

pedestal from .015' sheet styrene and position it according to the template. Detail each mounting plate corner with a Grand Line bolt head, Fig. 4.

Before assembling the bed walls, trim away the undersized upper wall lips (we'll correct this problem later) and sand off the mold marks, Fig. 5. I chose to exchange the M21 rear panel (part C5) for an M3 rear panel (part C28) to take advantage of the M3's external storage racks. Glue the wall panels to the floor assembly.

Cab assembly. Except for a few details, this assembly follows Steps 8 and 9 in the kit instructions. Passenger seats were removed to gain additional storage: Install only the driver's seat. Make a rearview mirror mount from stretched sprue. Do not install windshield glass—it was usually removed before it could be shot out.

Headlights. Use copper wire for headlight cables: Drill an .0145" hole in the bottom of each light's mounting bracket and super glue the wire in this hole. The wires enter the engine compartment via holes drilled in the fenders and wheel wells. On some half-tracks the headlight wiring passed through holes in the chassis frame.

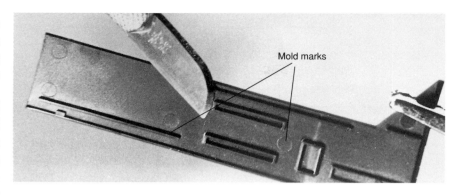

Fig. 5. Based on extensive research, Hilber noted that for later-model M3s, the interior of the walls is more accurate without the raised lips along the edges. Certainly the walls look better without factory mold marks!

Jerry cans. Gas cans are supplied in the kit, but I preferred Verlinden 1/35 scale jerry can holders and Italeri 1/35 scale U.S. jerry cans. Italeri jerry cans must be trimmed slightly to fit. Use lead foil for tie-down straps, and a loop of copper wire for cinch rings, Fig. 6. Thread a lead-foil strap end through the completed buckle, bending it over just enough to grip the ring, and secure it with super glue. Wrap the strap around a gas can, bend the end of the strap back to cinch it tight, and secure the strap with super glue.

Finishing the body. Combine the cab and bed, then install the other parts of the body: doors, side carrier racks, etc. Steve Zaloga's *U.S. Half-tracks of World War Two* (Osprey number 31) has excellent

overhead photos of the distinctive interior upper wall lip that joined and strengthened the armored sides and rear of M3 through M21 series APCs. The shape of the lip varied depending on vehicle model and manufacturer.

Some models (such as the M5) had triangular keystone supports at the corners—the M3 did not. This error in Tamiya's otherwise accurate kit is easily remedied: Glue .020" x .080" strip styrene along the top inside edges of all walls, including the cab doors and windshield, Fig. 7.

Tiny details. Drill mounting holes for the tarp mounts, but don't install the mounts. They were removed to allow traverse of the 107 mm mortar. Stow a few storage boxes: You can use toolboxes from

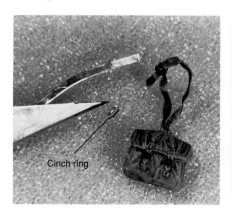

Fig. 6. Copper wire and lead foil make realistic belts and buckles.

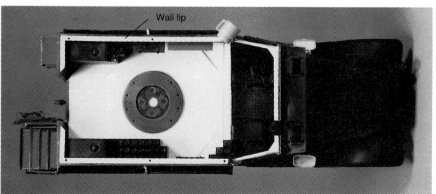

Fig. 7. Wall lips, M3-style: A good material to use for these distinctive strips is strip styrene.

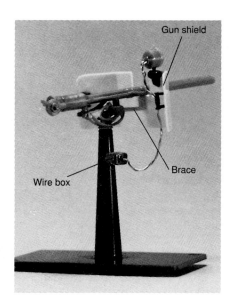

Gun shield

Brace

Wire box

Fig. 8. Vietnam-era half-tracks featured field-fitted armament. Hilber detailed a recoilless rifle with copper wire, scraps of plastic, sheet styrene—and ingenuity.

the M3 kit, or build your own from .015" styrene. They look better if they're dented and weathered.

Battle-damage patches are a nice touch. Make the patches from .015" styrene, and add thin beads of epoxy putty around the edges for weld lines.

An M60 machine gun was usually fixed to a pintle on the cab's passenger side. Use an M3 gun mount (parts C13 or C41 and part C5) and glue it to the top edge of the windshield frame. You may have to trim the wall lip to get a good fit.

Heavy weapons. Tamiya's 1/35 scale 107 mm mortar and crew look good straight from the box. Tamiya's U.S. Infantry Weapons set provides a better .50 caliber machine gun than the one supplied with the M21.

I armed my APC with a recoilless rifle, Fig. 8. Whichever weapon you choose, an improvised armored gun shield is a must: I've seen many different styles built in field machine shops. I made the shield from .015" sheet styrene, and attached it to the rifle mount using a scrap of sprue for a brace. Splitting a .50 caliber machine gun handle (M21 kit part C20 or Weapons Set part 58) makes good shield grab handles. Bore out the rifle barrel ends (parts 16 and 18) with an .039" bit. Detail with more Grandt Line nuts and bolts.

My veteran friend recommended fitting searchlights on the vehicle. I scratchbuilt these using model car parts. Copper wires run from the searchlight to a scrap-plastic electrical box on the bed floor.

Final construction and details. Join the chassis and body assemblies, then attach the weapons. You can use the radio gear and antenna stay from the M21 (parts Z11-16 and C3). Detail the handset with a phone cord of copper wire. Attach the antenna stay on the wall lip near the cab, run a copper wire antenna cable from the stay to the radio console, then make the antenna from stretched sprue.

Vietnam half-tracks rarely traveled light. Pile up plenty of sandbags on the cab and bed floors (an anti-mine measure); stow as much ammunition as possible (half-track crews used a lot of it, often simply for "recon by fire"); and don't forget extra canteens!

I used the ammo boxes from the M3 and M21 kits; the rangefinder tripod comes from Tamiya's M577 kit (parts D9-11). H-R Products' white-metal M16, Car-15, and M60 look great.

A final note on paint schemes and markings: American APCs in Vietnam wore olive drab that faded rapidly in the harsh climate. Many crews painted over the white U.S. recognition star to avoid giving enemy gunners a "bullseye." At the same time, less cautious crews displayed extravagant graffiti. One vet said he removed slogans from his gun shield because he figured he was drawing too much fire. He repainted them later when he realized *everyone* was drawing too much fire.

REFERENCES
• Arnold, James, *The Illustrated History of the Vietnam War: Armor*, Bantam Books, New York, 1987
• Dunstan, Simon, *Armor of the Vietnam Wars*, Osprey Publishing, London, 1985
• Zaloga, Steven, *U.S. Half-tracks of World War Two*, Osprey Publishing, London, 1983

SOURCES
• Styrene sheet and strips: Evergreen Scale Models, 12808 N. E. 125th Way, Kirkland, WA 98034
• Detail nuts and bolts: Grandt Line Products, 1040B Shary Court, Concord, CA 94518
• White-metal detail parts: H-R Products, P.O. Box 67, McHenry, IL 60050

BUILDING A PAIR OF 1/35 SCALE TANK DESTROYERS

Gunning for big game—the M10 (top) and M36 (bottom) have a lot in common, especially from a modeler's point of view.

BY COOKIE SEWELL

Sometimes technology passes old kits by—that's what happened to my out-of-production 1/35 scale Sherman tank destroyers, a Tamiya M10 (No. MT 142) and an Italeri M36B1 (last available from Testor, No. 794). The Tamiya M10 was actually an M10A1 using an ancient M36 hull molding (approximately 1/31 scale) and a new 1/35 scale M10 turret. The Italeri kit had better proportions, but it was odd because so few M36B1s saw service. I chose to

build an M10 and M36 instead.

The M10 and M36 have many interchangeable parts. The M10 uses spoke idlers and "lace work" drivers with solid wheels, and the M36 features solid idlers and disk drivers with spoked road wheels. Since Testor/Italeri's Sherman family has spoked idlers and Tamiya's M10 has solid wheels, you can swap them. As for scratch-building the hulls, both feature straight lines and simple angles, easy to cut from sheet styrene. Also, the scratchbuilt portion is the same for both—the M10A1

drawings in Steven Zaloga's book, *U.S. Tank Destroyers of WWII* (see REFERENCES) provide armor-plate angles for the hull.

Allow for sheet-styrene thicknesses when measuring outside

SHEET-STYRENE CONVERSION TABLE	
.010"	= .25 mm
.015"	= .375 mm
.020"	= .5 mm
.025"	= .625 mm
.030"	= .75 mm
.040"	= .1 mm

Fig. 1, M10 — Cut off fenders / Italeri
Italeri / Tamiya / Italeri

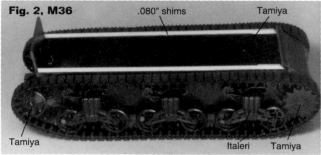

Fig. 2, M36 — .080" shims / Tamiya
Tamiya / Italeri / Tamiya

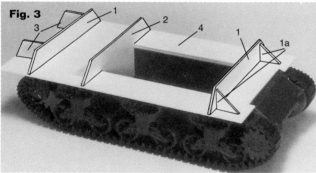

Fig. 3 — 3 / 1 / 2 / 4 / 1 / 1a

Fig. 4 — 5a only

Bevel

1
(2x)
Front
and
rear
supports

7

Front plate

9
(2x)

10
(2x)

3
(2x)
rear

2
Fire wall

dimensions. Although these sizes often are labeled in inches, I find it easier to measure construction in millimeters. Consult the conversion table to keep things straight.

The bottom. Use the Italeri hull for the M10 (Fig. 1). Cut fenders flush with the sides (the photo shows fenders before removal). Sand off doors on the rear plate and fill all holes. Smooth the backs of the Tamiya bogies. Fudge their position on the lower hull; it's easier than converting them to the correct height. Install Italeri idlers and idler adjusters, and driver wheels with "lace" disks rather than solid ones, then add other lower-hull details and tracks.

For the M36, use the Tamiya hull and Italeri bogies (Fig. 2). Trim 3 mm from the wide end of the exhaust pipes to fit them under the hood to be added later. Correct the height of the hull with .080" styrene strip. Use plastic scraps and Squadron Green Putty to fill gaps and smooth the lower hull.

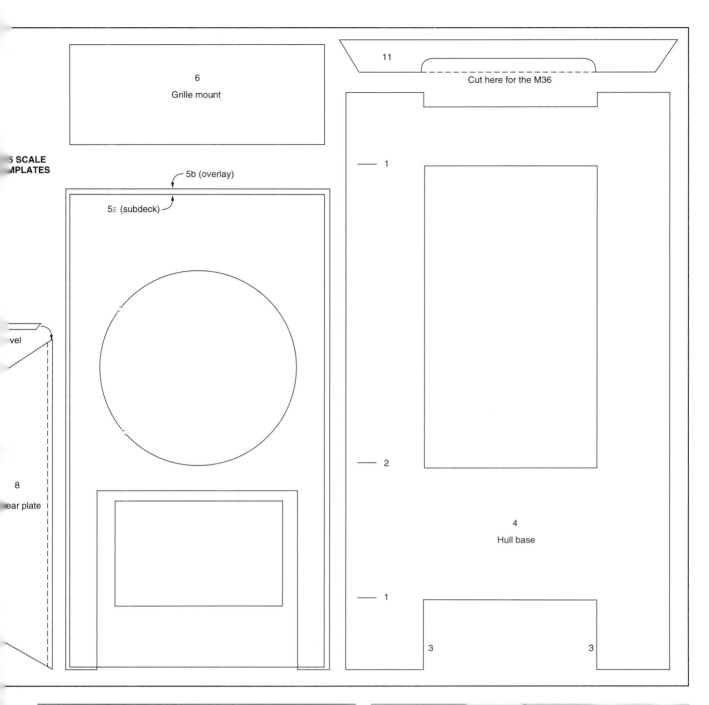

6
Grille mount

SCALE
MPLATES

5b (overlay)

5a (subdeck)

vel

8

ear plate

11

Cut here for the M36

1

2

4
Hull base

1

3

3

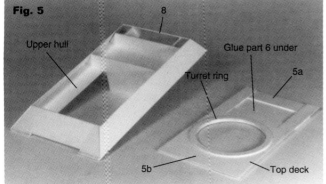

Fig. 5

8

Upper hull

Glue part 6 under

5a

Turret ring

5b

Top deck

Fig. 6

7

Reverse bevel

9

Resin transmission housing

99

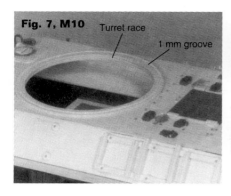

Fig. 7, M10 Turret race 1 mm groove

Fig. 8, M36 11 10

Fig. 9, M10 11 10 Exhaust cutout

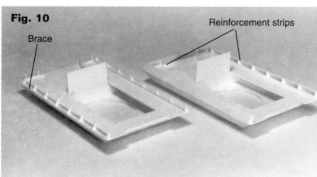

Fig. 10 Brace Reinforcement strips

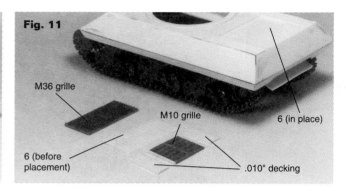

Fig. 11 M36 grille M10 grille 6 (in place) 6 (before placement) .010" decking

The hull. The only differences in the scratchbuilt parts of the two are in engine decks and lower rear panels. Cut sheet styrene according to the templates on pages 98 and 99. Cut template part 4 from .040" sheet, and parts 1, 2, and 3 from .030" sheet. Trim part 2, the fire wall (Fig. 3), to get a good fit—each hull differs slightly. Brace the fire wall with triangular scraps.

Rear part 1 is braced by parts 3. Glue parts 3 to the inside edges of part 4, and parts 1a to the top outer corners of front part 1. Check your work with a square.

Cut out the top decks: Part 5a is subdecking, made from .040" sheet; 5b is the top decking (.010" sheet). Why two layers? Because the kit parts are .050" thick. Also, the 1 mm top-sheet overlap makes a smoother joint. Fig. 4 shows part 5a without the 5b overlay. Fig. 5 shows the M36 top deck with part 5b in place.

Cut part 6 and glue it under the rectangular opening in part 5a

(Fig. 5). This will be the mount for the engine grille.

Parts 7, 8, and 9 are cut from .040" sheet. Bevel part 8's long sides toward each other. Bevel part 7 the same way, except on the dotted line where it meets the transmission housing (Fig. 6); there it's beveled in the opposite direction. Position parts 8 and 9 with the top bevel above parts 1.

Fig. 6 shows the transmission housing. I replaced the kit part with a Chesapeake Model Designs late-Sherman resin casting (part No. 10).

Glue parts 9 to the sides. Don't bevel; glue the top sides even with the tops of the front and rear upper plates. That should leave about 1 mm around the top to accept the decking. Test fit and trim to fit, but leave it off for now.

Turret race and lower body. The turret race is a 66 mm disk with a cutout to match each turret: 52 mm for the M10, 51 mm for the M36. Fig. 5 shows the

completed M36 race in place. To replicate the bullet splash plate on the M10 race, cut a 1 mm-wide groove in the race 1 mm in from the edge (Fig. 7).

For the lower body, cut parts 10 and 11 from .030" sheet; bevel the edges that fit against the hull. Cut along the dotted line of part 11 for the M36, the solid line for the M10 (Fig. 8 and 9). The M10 rear-hull cutout is for the exhaust system.

Parts 10 and 11 require angled bracing made from .040" sheet, 7 mm high, 4 mm deep, and mounted 1 mm in from the edge (Fig. 10). Each hull gets 20 braces. Side braces are reinforced at their lower back edges by 20 mm-long .040" x .080" styrene strips, the two rear braces by similar 12 mm-long segments of .040" x .080" strip.

Grilles. You'll need kit-supplied engine decks—use Tamiya's M4A3, or Italeri's M4A2 or M36B1. Cut the grille and its

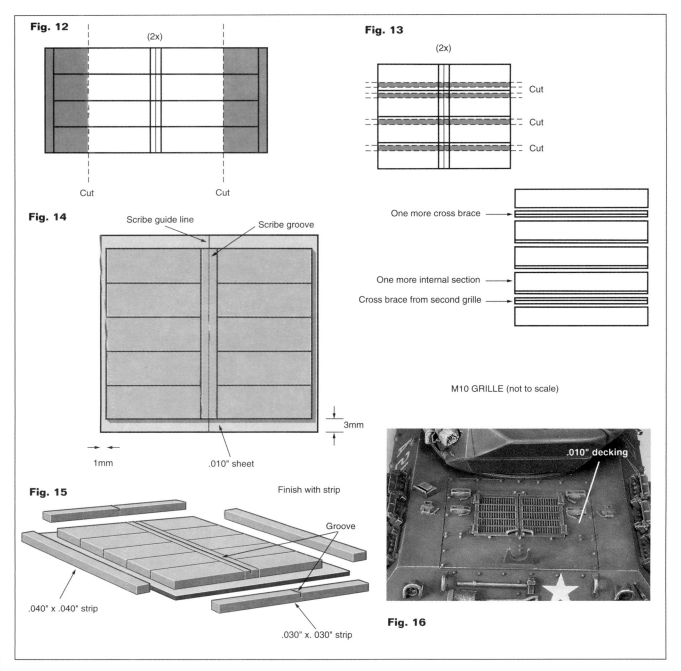

Fig. 12

(2x)

Cut   Cut

Fig. 13

(2x)

Cut

Cut

Cut

One more cross brace →

One more internal section →
Cross brace from second grille →

M10 GRILLE (not to scale)

Fig. 14

Scribe guide line

Scribe groove

3mm

1mm   .010" sheet

Fig. 15

Finish with strip

Groove

.040" x .040" strip

.030" x. 030" strip

.010" decking

Fig. 16

frame from the kit part. Fig. 11 shows the grilles and grille inset on the hull.

The grille cutout drops right onto the M36. However, the M10 grille is not as wide and has five sections per door. You'll need three kit grilles for this.

Cut two grilles to 25 mm wide (Fig. 12). Separate the sections laterally to get four 25 mm-wide sections from one grille and one from the other (Fig. 13). Slice off one cross brace from the second grille section, then trim and sand to even up the parts. Cut an .010" sheet 26 mm long and 27 mm wide (Fig. 14) and scribe a guideline in the center. Align one long grille edge 3 mm from the sheet edge, then glue the sections in place on the sheet. There should be a 3 mm tab at each end and a 1 mm tab on each side; don't cut them off.

Finish the grille with strip styrene (Fig. 15). Use .040" x .040" strip for the outside edges and .030" x .080" for the ends. Groove the end tabs to replicate door flaps. Use .010" sheet for decking around the grille (Figs. 11 and 15).

Exhausts. My M10 has an exhaust system from a Tamiya M3 Lee (kit No. 35039). Using .040" x .080" strip, cut a deflector-plate mount as wide as the hull rear, and two

.040" x .080" strip

13

9.5 mm

14

Fig. 17, M10

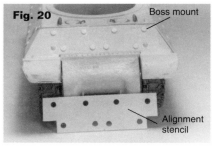

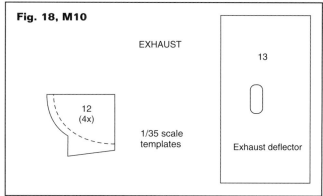

Fig. 18, M10

EXHAUST

13

12
(4x)

1/35 scale
templates

Exhaust deflector

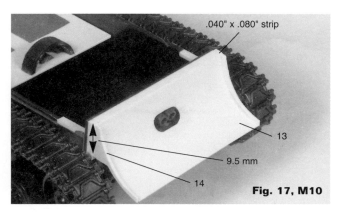

Fig. 19, M36

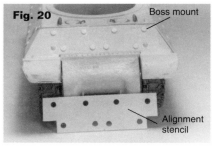

Boss mount

Alignment
stencil

Fig. 20

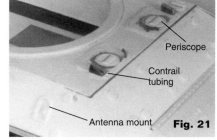

Periscope

Contrail
tubing

Antenna mount

Fig. 21

9.5 mm-long pieces. Mount these on the kit's rear hull plate (Fig. 17). Cut out four parts 12 and one part 13 from .010" sheet (Fig. 18). Trim two parts 12 along the dotted line; curl part 13 around a knife handle. These are the insides of the exhaust deflector. Two more parts 12 glued to the outside of part 13 complete the duct. I made an M36 deflector from a spare part and sheet styrene (Fig. 19), but M4A3 kit parts work too.

Hull details. I produced 1/8" styrene disks with a leather punch

for appliqué-armor boss mounts, aligned them with a stencil made from .040" sheet (Fig. 20) and topped them off later with Grandt Line hex nuts.

For hatch periscopes, punch out 1/4" disks of .020" sheet and feather into the hatch with putty and sanding (Fig. 21). An .010" disk forms the periscope base, and .010" strip works for the cover. Make hinges from Contrail tubing scraps cut into three sections and sanded to shape.

Drill a 3/16" hole in the side of the hull where the antenna mount

goes (Fig. 21), then cut it to shape. Wrap .010" sheet around a paintbrush handle and glue it in place to form the mount's back wall. The floor is .020" scrap. Cut .020" sheet to form the mount's cast edge.

Make new grouser racks from styrene strip. Form vertical channels by gluing two .010" x .040" strips on either side of an .020" x .030" strip and cut to length: four 13 mm and two 16 mm. Each lateral rail is a 50 mm-long section of .020" x .080" strip. Fig. 22 shows an empty rack.

Fig. 22

Grouser
rack

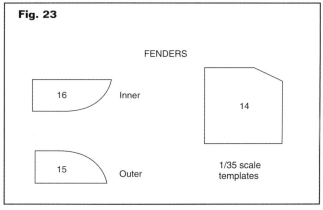

Fig. 23

FENDERS

16   Inner

14

15   Outer

1/35 scale
templates

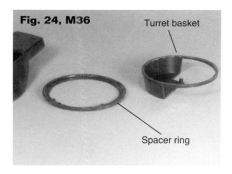
Fig. 24, M36

Turret basket

Spacer ring

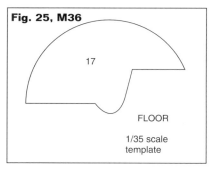
Fig. 25, M36

17

FLOOR

1/35 scale template

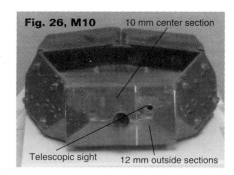
Fig. 26, M10

10 mm center section

Telescopic sight

12 mm outside sections

Fig. 27, M10

.010" sheet and strip

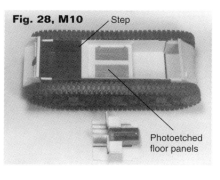
Fig. 28, M10

Step

Photoetched floor panels

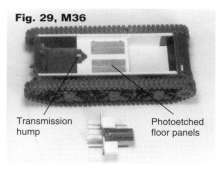
Fig. 29, M36

Transmission hump

Photoetched floor panels

Each fender comprises one part 14, one part 15, and one part 16, cut from .010" sheet (Fig. 23). Curl part 14 and cement parts 15 and 16 in place on part 14. Detail the fender with .010" x .030" strip and scrap-plastic braces. Taillights are spare Sherman parts with two modified Italeri M4A1 horn guards for protective braces. My Sherman spares box provided stowed equipment.

Turret. The M36 turret needs corrections: It has an inaccurate basket and sits about 2.5 mm too high. Cut the spacer ring and basket away from the turret (Fig. 24). This photo shows the turret basket partially cut to shape; the floor you want is provided as part 17 (Fig. 25). Attach it with three

13 mm-long .020" x .010" braces.

The M10 mantlet is too wide. Use a miter box and saw a 10 mm-wide section from the center of the mantlet (Fig. 26). Trim each outside section to 12 mm wide by cutting off the inside edges. Sand mating surfaces smooth and glue it back together, smooth seams with putty and sanding, then drill a 2 mm hole for a telescopic sight to the left of the gun.

Cut back the sides of the gun mount from the outside of the turret, plate them over with .010" sheet, and use .010" strip to fill the gap (Fig. 27).

Fighting compartment. The M10 has an M4A2 floor (Fig. 28), and the M36 has an M4A3 floor (Fig. 29). Use .040" shims to mount

new floors. The floor is hull width, 48 mm long, and butts the fire wall. There is a step at the rear of the M10 floor, about 6 mm long and 3 mm high, to clear the transmission. The M36 has a car-like hump instead.

Replicate floor panels with On the Mark photoetched two-panel doors. Glue an electrical junction box in the center of the fire wall and a rack-shaped cooler on the right to help fill in the compartment.

Detail the M36 with canteens and a fire extinguisher on the left side, a telescopic sight behind the mantlet, an elevation wheel, and a breech block from a big chunk of styrene (Fig. 30). The M10 also can use one (Fig. 31).

Fig. 30, M36

Breech block

Fig. 31, M36

Breech block

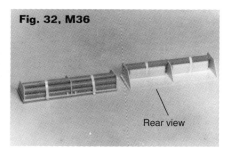
Fig. 32, M36

Rear view

Because both used "shoot and scoot" tactics to avoid direct engagements, they stowed few shells in their ready racks—six in the M10, 11 in the M36. The rest were in shipping tubes. Ready racks are hard to see inside the turret; make them from scraps of sheet and strip styrene (Fig. 32). Make seats from scrap styrene and add control rods. Make a transmission hump from .010" sheet rolled over sprue. The transmission I slapped together combines old Bandai 1/48 scale engine blocks and a jet engine from a Monogram Me 262.

Adding .010" interior walls eased painting and smoothed the fit. I used .010" x .030" flashing around the floor and fire-wall joints. Personal gear stowed on turret exteriors includes rolls and bags made from wrapping-tissue paper. The gear is attached with .005" straps.

Paint. Figs. 33 and 34 show both vehicles before painting. Fit parts to detect gaps, then dismantle for painting. Using Floquil lacquers, paint the interior primer gray and overspray with reefer white. Mask the interior and spray the outsides with a base coat of RLM 73 dark green and overspray with AN 613 olive drab. Apply a thin black wash and dry-brush with light yellow. After painting the tracks rust and overspraying with grime, give them a thin black wash and dry-brush with Rub 'n Buff silver leaf.

Markings place my tank destroyers in Europe in 1944: the M10 with the 702nd Tank Destroyer Battalion (Fig. 35), and the M36 with the 704th Tank Destroyer Battalion (Fig. 36). I made the codes on the fenders by rubbing dry transfers onto clear decal film.

REFERENCES

• Balin, George, *D-Day Tank Battles: Beachhead to Breakout,* Arms and Armour Press, London, 1984
• Hunnicutt, R.P., *Sherman: A History of the American Medium Tank,* Presidio Press, Novato, California, 1978
• Zaloga, Steven, *Patton's Tanks,* Arms and Armour Press, London, 1984
• Zaloga, Steven, *U.S. Tank Destroyers of WWII,* Arms and Armour Press, London, 1985

SOURCES

• Squadron Green Putty: Squadron Mail Order, 1115 Crowley Drive, Carrollton, TX 75011-5010
• Photoetched floor panels: On the Mark Models, P.O. Box 663, Louisville, CO 80027
• Sheet, rod, and tube styrene: Plastruct, 1020 S. Wallace Place, City of Industry, CA 91748
• Resin transmission housing: Chesapeake Model Designs, available from Baseline Hobbies, 105 Main St., Mineola, NY 11501
• Detailing nuts and bolts: Grandt Line Products, 1040B Shary Court, Concord, CA 94518
• Contrail rod and tubing: available from Imported Specialties, 3655 Sullivan Ave., Columbus, OH 43228

Fig. 35, M10

Fig. 36, M36